PERGAMON

Tevhit Kekeç
Archeologist, researcher in Bergama Museum

HİTİT COLOR
KARTPOSTAL SANAYİ TİCARET VE PAZARLAMA LİMİTED ŞİRKETİ
Cağaloğlu Yokuşu, Çele Han No. 39 İstanbul Tel: 526 56 51 - 520 78 49

Photographs:
Turhan Birgili
German Archeology Institute - Elisabeth Steiner
E.Sabri Yurdakul
Cemal Mermer
Erken Fotoğraf Stüdyosu

Graphic Design: Melih Öndün
Drawings: Gürbüz Polat
Translation: Murat Uçaner
Typesetting: Patrol Ajans
Color Seperation, Mounting and Printing: CEKA Matbaacılık

HİTİT COLOR İstanbul   ISBN 975-7487-01-5

COVER: Smiling Child (Eros), 2 nd Century A.C.

CONTENTS

NAME, ESTABLISHMENT AND ITS HISTORY

Pergamon is one of the most important ancient culture centers, which was established in West Anatolia, to the north of the plain Bakırçay runs through.

Its altitude is about 60 m. (The Acropolis had an altitude of 335 m.) Bakırçay stretches to the east-west direction in West Anatolia and it is one of the subsidence areas in the region which is filled with aluvial soil. Throughout history, this land and the region has always been chosen as a settlement place due to the favourable environmental conditions and due to the fertility mother nature has bestowed to its land.

Bakırçay which gives its name to the region, has had 3 periods:

First Period: Bakırçay used to reach the sea at a point which was quite close to the antique Pergamon settlement area.

Second Period: At this period, Bakırçay had to change its path and started flowing to the sea near Dikili, when the Pergamon sea was completely filled up as a result of heavy flows and subsidences.

Third Period: When the aluvial soil, carried by Boğazasan stream, filled up the mouth of Bakırçay, the river made itself a new path through. This new path reached the sea passing by Karadağ and through the natural bridge between Maltepe and Çandarlı. Bakırçay left this path at the beginning of the Christian Era. In his book "Geography", Strabon stated that Bakırçay used to flow, in the region, from the north of Karadağ. Plutarchos stated that Bakırçay was at first named after the son of Emeios and Kirois, threw himself into the river upon unwillingly killing the son of one of the Mysian rulers, it was called the stream of Kaikos. At present, the stream is called Bakırçay due to its path which passes near Bakırköy to enter the Kırkağaç plain.

Pergamon was called as Pergamon or Pargames in Greek, and as Pergamum or Pergamus in Latin. "Perg", "Berg" and "Ama" are roots which are often encountered in Anatolian languages (Perg means a castle). There are different myths for the establishment and the name of Pergamon.

According to a myth, the younger son of Neoptolemus and Andromache, the brave Pergamos came to Asia Minor and fought against the King of Teutrania for the rule. He killed the king and gave his name to the city.

In another myth, it is told that following the death of the King of Teutronia, Telles, the neighbouring rulers had found the opportunity to attack his heir, Euripilos who, in turn, called his friend Pergames for help. Pergames and his friends fought against the invaders and won the war. After victory, two cities are founded, namely Pergamos and Gyneion.

As it can be understood from the myths, the name Pergamon comes from Pergamos. (Pausanias states that the tomb of Pergamon's mother, Andromache, can be found to the south of the Soma highway, in Yığmatepe, and that the place is called "Andromachon")

The mythological story of Pergamon's legendary founder, Telephos, will be explained in the following pages together with the Altar of Zeus.

PREHISTORICAL ERA: The treasures discovered in the course of excavations in the Acropolis prove that the settlement story of Pergamon dates back to the Prehistorical period.

One of the two stone axes discovered during the excavations, on the big door of Acropolis, is made of hand stone, whereas the other one is of flint stone and is chipped on the surface. Although not belonging to the layer they were found in, these treasures can be said to prove the fact that there was some kind of a Prehistorical settlement in Pergamon.

The comparison of the materials of Yontan culture and of the ceramics which were found quite close to Pergamon, in Değirmentepe, brings about the fact that the settlement story of Pergamon dates back to 3.000 B.C.

Panoramic Reconstruction of Bergama (From the drawing of Bohn and Koch, 1886)

ARCHAIC AND CLASSICAL ERAS

At the end of 1930, some ceramic pieces belonging to the archaic period were discovered in the course of construction of the highway to Acropolis. The excavations made in the following years proved that Pergamon was a settlement area, in the archaic period. Kapıkaya, in the vicinity of Pergamon, is important due to the fact that it possesses treasures belonging to this period.

Persians had 4 great satraps in Ionia, Hellespont, Cilicia and Lydia. In Asia Minor, the lands under the rule of these satraps were rebelling against Persians. These rebellions caused uneasiness in the region, especially in Pergamon. The fear and the disgust of war were so great that they were immortalized in Pergamon works of sculpture.

The first historical registration about Pergamon was found in Xenophon. When Xenophon came to Pergamon, on his return from east Anatolia, the widow of Gongylos I, Hellas hosted him. Gongylos I was ruling the land at that time. Upon Hella's wish, Xenophon attacked and captured the castle of the Persian feudal lord Asidates (399 B.C.)

In 362 B.C., Orontes, the satrap of Mysia, lead a revolt against Persians; he, in time, withdrew his army to Acropolis and lived there until 354 B.C.. However, he had to give up when the Persian king Artaxenxes moved to Acropolis.

In 334 B.C., Alexander the Great crossed the Dardanelles and came to Asia Minor. There the governor of Pergamon showed respect to him. Thus, the Persian rule in Anatolia which lasted for 213 years came to an end, and a new period started in the history of Pergamon.

THE AGE OF ALEXANDER THE GREAT (356-323 B.C.)

When Alexander became the king of Macedonia after his father Philippos II, he was merely 20 years old (336 B.C.). In 334 B.C., he crossed Dardanelles and came to Anatolia, and fought against the Persian King Denios III. He won the war and ended the Persian rule in Asia Minor. When Western Anatolia came under his rule, Alexander chose Barsine, the widow of the Persian commander Memmon, to administer Pergamon.

In a short period of 10 years, Alexander conquered many places. When he died in Babylon, he was just 33 years old. (323 B.C.)

Before his death, Alexander was asked of his reign. "The one who is the most suitable for this position will rule the empire ".Upon these words, his generals started to fight against each other. At the end, the empire was divided among his generals. Seleukos received Syria, Mesopotamia and East Anatolia; Lysimachos received South and West Anatolia, and Kasandros received Greece and Macedonia.

One of the commanders, Antigonos conquered Anatolia and tried to fulfil his aim of capturing all the lands in the Empire. Realising the danger this may cause, Lysimachos, Seleukos - the Syrian King-, Kasandros and Ptolomaios - the Egyptian King-made an allience for fighting against him. The wars continued from 315 B.C. to 301 B.C..During these wars, Pergamon was first captured by Antigonos, and then was left to Lysimachos.

Realising the strategic location of Pergamon, Lysimachos turned it into a military base and brought his treasure of 9000 talent gold coins, here. He, then, entrusted his treasure to the Paphlogonialian officer, Phileteiros. Upon ensuring the expansion of the kingdom from Thrace to the Tonos mountains, Lysimachos established diplomatic relations with his allies and favored marital ties between royal families. He, therefore, married Amastris, one of the daughters of Persian Oscartes. Then, he left her to marry Arsinoe, the daughter of the Egyptian King, Ptolemaios I. This was a political marriage, in the sense that there were 40 years between the bride and the groom.
When they got married Ansinoe was only 20 years old, whereas Lysimachos was almost 60 (299 B.C.).

Lysimachos was a person who gave importance to constructions. Thus he gave the order to build a new city for his wife Arsinoe, in Ephesus. The ruins which are visited today in Ephesus are the ruins of that city. As he got older, Lysimachos became suspicious of everything and everyone. Arsinoe made him believe that Agatokles, his son from his first wife, would have his throne, and so he had him murdered (284 B.C.).
The event caused riots in the army and among the people who really loved Agatokles. Because of the fear and unrest, Agathokles' brother, widow and children took refuge in Syrian king Seleukos. Also, Philetairos, the commander of the castle of Pergamon, secretly communicated with Seleukos and told him that if he agreed to fight against Lysimachos, he would give the treasury to Seleukos. Seleukos accepted the offer and attacked Lysimachos. The two armies met at Koroupedion, near Sardes and fought with each other. Lysimachos died, and the war was won by Seleukos. The dead body was taken back to the capital of the kingdom, Lysimakhia, where it was buried with ceremonies.

The Vaulting Bottom Galleries of Traian Temple

THE PERIOD OF KINGDOM

PHILETAIROS (283-263 B.C.)

After the death of Lysimachos, Philetairos, the commander of the castle of Pergamon, refused to part the deal with Seleukos. He did not give the coins to him, but had the likeness of Seleukos impressed, there by showing his allegiance to him. Then he sent expensive presents to the neighbouring princes to establish friendly relations.He, then, bought a very expensive land from the Syrian king. When the Egyptian king was killed on the way to Thrace, by Kereunos, Philetairos sent his corpse to the new Syrian king, Antiokhos, the son of Seleukos. Thus, he showed his respect once again.

When Antiokhos left the city to fight against enemies, Philetairos took a deep breath. First, he increased the means of security in the city and then replaced the old coins with the new ones. On one side of the coins there was his name and portrait and on the other side there was his shield spear, helmet and Goddess Athena's figure.

Until 263 B.C., Philetairos used his treasure for construction in and around Pergamon; he built a temple in honour of Anatolia's main goddess Kybele, in Memurt castle (Kınık), 20 km. south of Pergamon; another in the name of Apollon inAegean castle, and one to the honour of Demeter in Acropolis. He also gained respect and allies from neighbouring cities by sending presents. From an inscription found in Kysikos, it is learned that Kysikonians organized festivals each year to the honour of Philetairos.

From an inscription found in his garden in Greece, it is understood that he used to send great presents to Delphoi Holy Land. Delphoilians accepted the brothers of Philetairos, Attolos and Eumenes as formal visitors. (An inscription in Delos island writes about his war against Galats, the victory and the Galatian's exile to further places.)

Philetairos adopted his nephew, Eumenes I, since he did not any children of his own. After his death in 263 B.C., Eumenes I became the prince.

EUMENES I
(263-241 B.C.)

Antiochos, not accepting Eumenes I as the prince who succeeded Philetairos, wanted the treasury back. Eumenes I did not accept this offer and made his preparations for a possible war. By watching the Syrian king's

Acropolis Library

military acts in Sordeis, he thought that they could be dangerous. Thus, he attacked Sardes with his army and defeated Antiochos's army. Antiochos, while escaping, died on the road (262 B.C.). Eumenes I, after this victory, enlarged his frontiers. He restored the Bergama Acropolis and built new castles in the frontiers. Among them, Philetairia, placed at the sides of Ida (Kazdağı) mountain, and Attolei, placed in Lydia are important. (Philetaria castle took its name from Philetairos. Since this city was founded by Eumenes I, a castle was built in his honour.)

Eumenes I, abiding to Philetairos' politics, kept and strengthened his friendship with many cities and sites. He was loved by the people for his success in governmental work. In an inscription found in Bergama, Eumenes requests the public to choose Strategoses again. He also wanted the public to appreciate the Strategoses[1] by giving wreaths to them during the Panathenaia festivals made in Athens every four years.

This condition resulted from Strategoses' governing Pergamon in a good way by preventing abuses. The public, to show their gratefulness to Eumenes, elected Strategoses again. They also accepted giving wreaths to them, which was a quality of people who made the highest duties to the country.

Their sacrificing on behalf of the public was also accepted. The public, in order to show their gratefulness to their king Eumenes I, gave him the name "Eumenes Euergetes", which meant goodness loving Eumenes. In his period, Pergamon became one of the leading cultural centers, especially in art and in science. He also gave importance to sports and supported the young Attalos.

About this subject, a marble incsription gives us information. In this inscription it was written that:

"Many two-wheeled, many running chariots came from Cebel-i Lebanon [2] and Teselia. Among them Attalos" chariot was present, too. The chariots were lined behind a stretched rope. When the rope was withdrawn, the horses ran. Attalos "chariot was going ahead like an arrow, and was raising dust. His chariot won the race amid a shower of applause." This result awoke great joy in Pergamon. Speeches were given. In the contest, the epic story of the Pitonian poet, Arkesilos came first:

"Pergamon deserves praise not only for her weapons, but for her horses, too. If a mortal is allowed to quote the thoughts of Zeus, he may say Pergamon deserves more fame."

Eumenes I who was raised to the level of gods, after 22 years of governing, died in 241 B.C. Ktesikles claims his addiction for alcohol as the reason of his death.

ATTALOS I (241-197 B.C.)

After the death of Eumenes I, Attalos I took the throne. At this time, there were three Galatian tribes which divided Anatolia into three population groups. Pergamon was paying tax to one of the three Galatian tribes, Tolisgots, for keeping her frontiers in security. The Galatian Tolisgot tribe wanted the same tax from Attalos I, as well. Attalos I, not finding it appropriate to his honour and sovereignty, did not give the money and sent their ambassadors back. Because of Pergamon's not giving the tax, Tolisgot tribe started to go from the Ankyra region to Pergamon. Tolisgots came rather to were coming more for plunder the cities and rob Pergamon's treasury than to gain land. The two armies met at a place near Soma, in Kaikos, and started to fight.

At the beginning of the war the Pergamon army happened to be shaken, but after Attalos advices and his giving a votive offering to gods, all the attacks of Galats were

Acropolis Theater

defeated and their commanders were killed. Thus, the Kaikos war ended in victory (241 B.C.) The war equipments taken from the Galats were put into the Temple of Athena, in Acropolis. There, a statue of Athena was set up by Attolos I.

The people gave Attolos I the name Soter (Rescuer). They took him as a half god. Prince Attolos was declared king. As a sovereignty mark, the coins were printed, which cost 4 drahmis.[3] Galats, not accepting the defeat, wanted help from one of the tribes, Tektosogs. They also made the offer of joining to the Syrian king, Antiokhos Hierax who was living in Sardeis. In a year, they prepared themselves and attacked to Pergamon, but they lost this war (240 B.C.). The state of Seleukos was divided between Seleukos II (246-226 B.C.) and his younger brother Antiokhos Hierax who was living in Sardeis. When the two began to fight with each other between 235-284 B.C., Attolos, declared war against the Syrian king Antiokhos, Galatian Tektosogs and Tolistoogs. He conducted 3 wars following each other.

In the wars made in Sardeis-Koloe (229-228) and in Koria (228-227), he defeated the enemy. As a result, the cities of the state of Pergamon kingdom were stretching from Marmara to the Toros Mountains. To the eternal memory of these wars, a magnificient monument was set up in the Temple of Athena. The lower part of the monument was longer than 14 meters.

1-Strategos: Council of 5 attorneys, ruling Pergamon. They were elected each year by the People's council.

2-Cebil-i Lübnan: A free city which had the outskirts of Beyrut as borders.

3-There were the portrait of Athena and the portrait of Philatairos in the two successive sides of these coins.

While Attolos I was establishing a new order in the frontiers enlarged by the victories, he learned that the Syrian king Seleukos III (226-223 B.C.) passed over the

Toros mountains with his army which was commanded by Archaios. When this army entered Frigia, Seleukos was killed by a Galatian. After the death of Seleukos, Antiokhos III became the king. Antiokhos III (223-187 B.C.) asked Achaios to save the places that were taken by Attolos I. Achaios established Sardes as the center. He got back the places that were taken by Attolos I, up to the Toros Mountains, and established the Pergamon kingdom in the Kaikos domain. (219 B.C.) Achaios upheaval, threatening Anatolia, displeased Syrion and Pergamon kings. Thus, Antiokhos III and Attolos I made an alliance to fight against Achaios. After the wars that continued for four years, Achaios took refuge in the Sardeision castle and he was killed by his own soldiers.

After these wars Attolos I tried to have relations with the west. Pergamon starting from the time of Philetairos had had good relations with Greece and in various cases had helped them. When the Macedonian king Phillipos V (221-178 B.C.) moved into the lands belonging to the Aetolia Union, Pergamons took their place beside Aetolians.[4] They made an alliance between the Aetolia Union and Rome which was threatened by Hannibal. Since Pergamon was an ally of the Aetolia union, it had favourable relations with Rome (203 B.C.).

Until his death, Attolos I fought against Macedonian king Phillipos V. However, he could not live to see the victory of his allies and Phillipos' leaving Teselia.

Attolos I, during his 43 years of kingdom, constructed important buildings in Pergamon. The library in Pergamon was founded in his time, also the construction of Zeus' altar was started by him.

He had four sons from his Kyrikonian wife, Apollonia; Eumenes, Attolos, Philetairos and Athenoias. He died in 197 B.C. After his wife's death in 166 B.C., a temple was made in Teos for Apollonia and Attalos who successfully gained the respect of the people.

EUMENES II (197-159 B.C.)

Upon the death of Attalos I, his oldest son Eumenes II became the king. Being well awared of the refined politics his father pursued, he continued to have friendly relations with Rome. After the defeat of Philippos V, he left his land and only kept the Aegia island to himself. When the Sparta tyranne, Nalois threatened the Akhaia Unity, he went to help with his army. Following victory, a monument was built in honour of Athena Nikhonos. Eumenes II thought that Antiokhos III, the king of Seleucids, would be dangerous for Pergamon, thus he fought against Antiokhos III, together with Rome. The battle took place on the Manisa plain, and the Pergamene army won the war.

Eumenes II (190 B.C.) enlarged its borders to Bythinia and Cappadocia, thus the city became a part of the Pergamon Kingdom in Thrace. During his 38 years of reign, Eumenes II had been very successful in both military and state affairs. His reign was the golden age of Pergamon. Like his father, Attalos I, he enjoyed discussions with poets, artists. Pythias, the historian, and Menandros, the philosopher were his best friends. During his reign, Pergamon became a center for arts and sciences. Besides philosophy, mathematics, literature, and astronomy, practical sciences like mechanics, ship building, architecture, leather manufactering advanced considerably.

4- Aetolia is placed to the south of Corinth Bay. Aetolia Union was based on sovereignity. The basic aim was to defense the political rule against Macedonia.

A Detail from the Friezes of Zeus Altar

Eumenes II gave importance to construction. The Temple of Zeus was built during this period. The library founded by his father was enlarged and enriched. The library halls were embellished with monuments and were almost turned into a museum. Strobon states that he had built holy places and libraries since he was very fond of Pergamon they were restorated during his reign. Inside the city walls, also referred to as Eumenes walls, in Acropolis, he had built eye-catching monuments. The reign of Eumenes was the richest and the most powerful period in the history of Pergamon. In his late years, his brother Attalols II took care of state matters. Eumenes II died in 159 B.C.

ATTALOS II (159 - 38 B.C.) AND ATTALOS III (138 - 133 B.C.)

After the death of Eumenes II, his brother Attolos II ascended the throne. The only son of Eumenes II was only twelve years old then. When he became the king, Attalos II vas 61 years old, he was known as a strong and able administrator, especially knowledgeable in military affairs. For the sake of the country's welfare, Eumenes II

Traian Temple

wished his brother's marriage to his wife Stratonike. Thus his little son would have been raised as a powerful king. Attalos II remained faithful to his brother under any condition, and thus was called "Attalos Philadelphos" (brother lover). When he became the king, he first made the Cappadocian King Oropher descend the throne, and in his place made his brother-in-law, Ariarathes, the king.

The king of Bithynia, Prusias, caused border fights and asked Rome for help against Pergamon. The Roman Senate, however, found Prusias guilty in this manner, and agreed with Attalos. According to the treaty signed, neither side kept more

than 1000 soldiers along its borders. Taking advantage of the treaty, Prusias attacked Pergamon. Attalos II took refuge on the acropolis. Prusias looted the lower city and burned it down. He had the statue of Asklepios by the sculptor Pyromachus taken to Bithynia and said "You belong to my land, protect it."

Attalos II acted quite politically against Prusias, Rome supported him, other city kings such as Mithradotes, Arianhes and others came to help. Prusias, at the end, asked for a treaty. According to the treaty, Prusias was to withdraw within his pre-war borders and had to pay 500 Talents. (Attalos II took sides beside Rome in the war against a fake Philippos. Philippos lost the war against Pergamon and was captured)

Attalos II always favoured good relations with Rome, he had sent his son Attalos III to Rome and secured future relations. He worked a lot for public projects and helped other cities as well. His most important public work project was the cleaning of the Ephesus harbour; he had the bottom of the harbour scraped so that big ships could enter. During his 21 years of reign, he built many monuments of himself, of Eumenes II, of Philetairos and Athaneios. He also built a stoa in Athens and a building for artists in Dionysos.

Upon the death of Attalos II, his nephew ascended the throne. Attalos III did not get involved in the affairs of the state and let his trusted people administer. He was interested in biology, zoology. He was very much under the influence of his mother whom he valued deeply, he was therefore called as "Attalos Philameter", the mother love.

Ancient writers state that the King made researches on special natural drugs. Polybis writes that Attalos III made use of biology and zoology books for his researches on animals. The doctors used a chemical he had discovered to cure skin illnesses.

Since he was a hypocondriac, he planted poisonous rots in his garden and tried them on guilty and very sick people in order to find their antipoison. Attalos III also got involved in art projects. He made bronze figures. Bithinians, under the rule of their king Nikomedes invaded some cities under the rule of the Kingdom. Attalos III had therefore fought against Nikomedes.

When the Capadocian King, Ariarathes stole the treasure of the Zeus Temple, Pergamon demanded help from its King. Attalos III intervened, gave an end to riots and saved the treasures. Upon victory a statue of the King was placed aside those of Asklepion, The God of Health, in Asklepion. Asklepion was called "Asklepios, The King's Holy Place". On the sculpture, it was written "The son of Eumenes Soter, beloved King Attalo Philometer."

After the death of his beloved mother Stratonike, when his beautiful wife Berenike died, the King got deeply suspicious. He used to think these deaths were a result of poisoning and caused deaths of many.

Attalos III died while working on a statue for his mother. His death in 133 B.C. ended a reign of 5 years. Due to his will "Populus Romenus bonorum Meorum heres esto", the country went under the rule of the Romans.

5- Charles Texier states that Attalos II was poisoned. Attalos III was influenced by this poisining.

Sacred Square of Athena
Ancient Road

THE ROMAN PERIOD

In his will Attalos III bequeathed the kingdom to Rome. Riots started among the people. The rich people moved to other places to grant their possessions. The Pergamon folk who prefered fighting joined the army organized by Aristorikos, the illegal son of Eumenes II, half brother of Attalos III. Some of the cities joined the revolt, but cities like Colophon, Samos, Myndros resisted joining but were seized by force. A Roman army was sent to Anatolia. (Bithinian king Nikomedes, Capadocia king Arıorathes, Paphlaonia king Pylemenes took sides with Roma.) In 131 B.C., a Roman army under the command of Consul Licinius Crassus came to Anatolia, but was defeated by Aristorikos near Myrına. In 130 BC. another Roman army under the command of Consul Perperna came to Anatolia and defeated Aristorikos. He was then taken to Rome and was murdered there.

M.Aquillius who became the Co nsul in 129 BC came to Pergamon to organize affairs. The rioting cities were given heavy punishments. Some lands were divided among Kingdoms which took sides with Rome during the war, the remaining lands came under the rule of Rome and the first Roman state (Provincia Asia) was established. Many Pergomanian artists had left the country and went to Aphrodisias where they founded the school of Sculpture.

After the King of Pontus Mithradates' defeat against Romans, Pergamon which was used as a base during this war, continued being ruled by Rome. During the reign of Ceasar, Pergamon lived through one of its best times;however,was affected by the riots upon his death. In 40 BC, in the land division between Octavionus and Antonius, the lands to the east of the Empire, including Anatolia were left to Antonius.

It was most dishonoring for Pergamon to let its 200.000 valuable books given to Cleopatra, the queen of Egypt as a present of Antonius.

The victory of Actium gave an end to the Republic period and the period of peace and wellfare opened for Pergamon while visiting Anatolia, Augustus stayed in Pergamon and the people built a temple for Rome-Augustus upon his consent and made a statue of him.

During the reign of Emperor Tiberus (AD 14-37) Pergamon favored constructions, the city which was destroyed during earthquakes, was built over. Pergamon became first in a contest organized between the cities to built a temple for the Emperor. It was also decided to call the name of the emperor during the ritual ceremonies.

The emperor had started the construction process of the Traian temple in Pergamon Acropol (98-11) 7, but the temple was finished during the rule of emperor Hadrianus (117-138). The Serapion is also an example of this period.

The small temple in Acropol was built for Faustino, the wife of emperor Marcus Aurelius, during his reign (157-180). Also at this period, the famous doctor Claudıus Galenus was presented a medal by the emperor. On the medal it was engraved that it was a present from Antoninus, the emperor of Romans to Galenus, the emperor of doctors.

The plague swept through Pergamon in 166 AD. An inscription discovered near the Temple of Zeus states: "Oh, Great Zeus, chase away the epidemiç that is destroying the city of Asklepios."

During his return from the Thrace campaign, Emperor Caracalla had a serious accident in Gallipolu and came to Pergamon to be treated in the Asklepion. Following his recovery, in gratitude, he supported the temples in the city. He had the temple of Dionysos, located on the terrace of the

Emperor Hadrianus (up)
Emperor Caracalla (down)

theater, plated with marble. Pergamon was called Neokoros after the construction of temple of Augustus. It had the same honor also during the periods of Traianus and Caracalla. Caracalla called it "Proto Metropolis", the number one city. Although it was stated that Pergamon was the metropol on the coins during the Roman Period, this was not true. At this period the most important city was Ephesus.

Pergamon was destroyed immensely during the earthquakes at the time of emperor Valerianus I (253-260). When Diokletianus divided the Asia Province into smaller provinces, Pergamon became a part of the new Asia province. (284-305). One of the 4 metropols during the reign of Theodosias, the Great, was Pergamon.

Upon the division of the Empire in 395 AD, a new period started for Pergamon which then was under the rule of East Roman Empire.

THE BYZANTINE ERA (395 - 1306 AD)

Pergamon was called as "The throne of the Devil-Devil's Throne) by St. John, at the early stages of Christianity Pergamon was a center for many religions and emperor cultures. Christianity started to spread in Anatolia especially starting from III. century. During the period of emperor Decius (249-251), tortures made to people accepting Christianity caused reactions. Due to the political situation in Pergamon, one God religion was favored. One of the seven churches in Anatolia, established by St. Paul was in Pergamon.

In 313, the emperor Constantine, stated that Christianity was to be accepted as a free religion. In the reign of Theodosios, in 379 Christianity became the official religion.

In 12th century, Edremit, Pergamon and Khliara (6) regions were attacked by Turks. Manuel Komenos, the first, built city walls for security and Pergamon became a leading castle in Neokastra region.

When the Byzantine Empire was divided, Pergamon and the provincia Neocastri was given to Byzantine Latin Empire. They however could never possess this region. According to the treaty made between Herry (1206-1216) and Theodaros Laskarıs (1204, 1222) Neocastri province was accepted to be a part of Nikeia Empire.

In 1301, the emperor Mihail moved back to Bandırma upon defeat of General Musollon to Osman Gazi in Koyunhisar.

Starting from this period, Pergamon was ruled by Turks.

THE TURKISH PERIOD

Bergama, at the year of 1306, was captured by Karasioğulları, and after Balıkesir, became the second important center of Beylik (principality) of Karasi. (Karasi Bey

A Column Arch-Byzantine Period

(the prince) preferred to increase the Turkish population there, by setting Sarı Saltuk Turks who, escaping from Mogols, went under his protection and who had come from Dobruca under the rule of Ece Halil.) Named after Ece Halil, the Atmaca district was known as the Ece district during the period of Beylik of Karasi. Upon the death of Aslan Bey, the Beylik was divided into two parts. One of these parts the center of which was Balıkesir, came under the rule of Demirhan. This district, in Arabic sources, was called "Mamlakat Agira", due to the ancient names, "Agiros" or "Agiraus". The other district, the center of which was Bergama, was called "Mamlakat Marmara" in the same sources.

The famous traveller İbn Batuta (1304-1377) visited these places in 1333 and mentioned about them in his book of travels as:

"By setting our way the other day, we reached Bergama. Although it was a ruined city, the castle on the mountain was well-preserved." "The name of the ruler of the city is Yahşi Khan. The word Khan has the meaning of "Sultan" among them. Yahşi, however, means beautiful and good. He was on the plateau when we arrived at the city. As soon as he heard of our arrival, he sent us food and a dressing which was made in north."

Yahşi Khan, son of Karasi Bey, died in 1334 or 1336. Meanwhile, leaders of Karasi, namely Hacı İl Bey and Ece Bey, who were annoyed of Demir Khan's oppression, sent a message to Orhan Gazi. In that message, they stated that half of the country would be left to the Ottomans, provided that Orhan Gazi would make Dursun Bey the leader of the Principality. After that offer, Orhan Gazi and Dursun Bey assaulted to Balıkesir. Thereupon, Demir Khan took shelter in Bergama castle. In order to reconcile these two brothers, Dursun Bey and Demir Khan, Orhan Gazi sent DursunBey to Bergama. However, Dursun Bey was killed by an arrow thrown from the castle, as soon as he reached the fronts of Bergama castle. Worn out by this, Orhan Gazi assaulted to Bergama Castle and surrounded it.

Upon that besiegement, Demir Khan was obliged to give up. There after he was taken to Bursa where he died of plague a few years later. (1339) Bergama after the year of 1345 was bounded to the Ottoman Empire. After becoming a part of Ottomans, Bergama lost its importance as a castle. Thereupon the Turkish people who came down from plateaus, settled in the valley. After the Ankara war, Tamburlaine plundered Bergama, and according to Byzantian historians, put all the Turks and Greeks whom he could find in the city, to the sword. In 14th and 15th centuries, Bergama was developed and it began to widen to the Bakırçay plain. Mosques, medreses and inns were built in the city.

Under the rule of Ottomans, Bergama village was bounded to Sancak (subdivision of a province) of Balıkesir until 1868. In 1868, it was bounded to Manisa and in 1890, to İzmir.

Bergama, in 1919 was stricted to Greek occupation, but was taken back on 14.7. 1922 The town was inhabited by Turkish immigrants who came from Greece, in place of Greeks who either left Bergama with the Greek army or who later exchanged places to abide the Lausanne agreement.

Today, Bergama, being an important village of agriculture and tourism, has a distinguished place in Anatolian Archaeology.

6- Near Akhisar and Bakırköy.

Pergamon Acropolis

PERGAMON EXCAVATIONS

In 1868-1875, the railway engineer Carl Humann came to Bergama while traveling in West Anatolia, and visited Acropolis. A year later, when he was working in the construction of Dikili-Bergama railway, he made some investigations in Bergama. During these investigations, he by sending relief frieze and an inscription to Germany, had them investigated in Berlin. (The frieze was found to belong to the Zeus Temple) Alexander Conze, Museum Director in Berlin, supported Carl Humann to undertake the excavations in Bergama, and on 17.8.1877, he succeeded in taking permission to undertake the excavations in Bergama.

Zeus Altar friezes, some architectural pieces and some sculptural works which were found during these excavations were taken to Germany. Today, these works are being exhibited in the Pergamon Museum of Berlin.

The first period excavations which began in 1878, with the finding of the place of Zeus Altar, continued till 1886, under the direction of Alexander Conze, the Berlin Museum Director. During these excavations, Zeus Altar, Upper Agora, Theatre, Terrace and Dionysos Temple, Athena Sacred Area, Tranian Temple, King Palaces and pressured water ways were worked upon, and the topography of Bergama was investigated.

Second period excavations, undertaken between 1900 - 1913, were carried out in charge of Wilhelm Dorpfeld who uncovered Troia. In these excavations, Gymnasium, Hera Sacred Area, Old Mainroad, houses and shops were brought to light; in addition, studies in the tumuli around Bergama were made. With the World War I, excavations were subjected to a break and only after the establishment of the Turkish Republic, the third period excavations began in 1927 with the granted permission of Atatürk who gave importance to archaeology and history.

Third period excavation studies, between 1927-1938, were undertaken with the leadership of Theodor Wiegand who was supported by Erich Boehringer. In this period excavations, Arsenal buildings, Heroons temeors, Demeter Sacred Area, Musalla cemetery, Serapeion (Scarlet Courtyard) were explored. Meanwhile, in 1933, with the attempts of Osman Bayatlı and German Archaelogy Institute, the construction of the new museum building began; it was completed in 1936. President K.Atatürk came to Bergama during these third period excavations in 1934, and visiting Asklepion, he took information about studies. With the beginning of World War II, the excavations were again subjected to a break. During the excavations between 1957-1968, under the direction of Erich Boehringer, searching for Hikephorion in the Musalla Cemetermy, cleaning of Troian terrace and Asklepion Sacred Area, and restoration studies (Traianeum, Big Altar, Demeter Sacred Area, Romport Gate) were carried out. In 1969-1971, excavation studies concerning Asklepios Sacred Area came to an end, under the direction of Oscar Ziegenous; in addition to that, the theatre in Asklepion and the walls of the North Corridor were restored by Turkish architects during the same period.

Since 1972, Wolfgang Radt has been in

City Excavations 1988

Down City Excavation 1988 (Up)
The Archaic Stone Modiolus (Down)

charge of the excavations. City excavation studies which began in this period (in the middle part of Acropolis slide) still continue; besides, excavations are undertaken in the area of Kapıkaya, 5 kilometers northwest of Acropolis, in Kybele and Mithros Sacred Area. During the restoration studies of the Traian Temple vaulty galleries have been explored and studies carried out to put the architectural pieces, which belong to the building, to their original places are still going on. Again in this period, studies about the antique city's net of water were made.

Besides the excavations undertaken by the German Archaeology Institute in Bergama, other excavations in the north-west of Acrapolis, in Kestel are being undertaken in charge of Selahattin Erdemgil since 1977. In this excavation studies, antique Pergamon ceramic workshops have been explored. (These workshops brought up the fact that Bergama was an important center of ceramics during the Hellenistic and Roman periods) In these excavations, not only ceramic workshops, but also many cemeteries have been explored.

Arsenal

CITY WALLS AND THE DEVELOPMENT OF THE CITY

First, the hill at the top had been surrounded with the walls and fortified as a castle. Today, only a small part of this very old wall can be seen. The castle gate has also remained in the same place since the time it was built.

During Philetairos period (283-263 B.C.), city walls were widened towards the south, however upper city walls were preserved exactly. In the same period the city spread up to the area over Gymnasium, so that the Demeter Sacred Area remained before the city walls.

During the periods of Eumenes I and Attalos I, the city walls were not widened.

During the reign of Eumenes II, city walls were enlarged towards the plain that laid in south and west directions. The total periphery of the city walls reached 4 km. in this period, and the Temenos of Demeter and the new Gymnasium were also included within these walls. The settlement in this region was mainly inside the city walls which were built in the reign of Philetairos.

With the fortification made in the period of Eumenes II, the parts in west, south and east which had a strategical importance and which were subject to attacks have been strengthened. In this period, lots of gates and defence towers were added to the city walls. These towers were usually built on the corners, on different directions.

The main entrance door (named Eumenes Gate), placed southerly had a fortified courtyard. The furnished antique main road, beginning from Eumenes Gate, made a curve inside the city and reached the top castle gate at the north.

Until the Roman Empire period, no further enlargement in the city walls was made, but constructions continued inside the castle.

In the Roman Empire period the city spread all over the antique plain. Improvement began in the city during the glorious periods of Traian and Hadrian. In the Roman period, besides the new theatre, an Amphitheatre and stadium, the Serapion temple in the name of Egypt gods was built on the hills and slides at the south-west of Acropolis. Serapeion, known as the "Red Courtyard" today, also implies that the city spread towards the antique plain. Antique sources inform that the city had a population of 150.000, at the mids of the Empire period.

In late Roman period, the city again began to settle inside the borders of acropolis. Around it, a Roman wall was built by using antique materials again. This wall, following the Philetairos wall at the west, included Gymnasium and the Temenos of Demeter within its borders.

During the Byzantine period, city limits got smaller and the city settled back to the upper castle. The walls, seen on the north edge of the castle peak, which were built with plaited bricks and stones, were constructed from mixed materials. This went on till the VIIth or VIIIth centuries A.D. In 1333, İbn Batuta wrote in his book of travels that the castle was sound.

During the Ottoman period, when Orhan Gazi invaded Bergama, the upper castle was used by Demirhan of Karasioğulları.

Pergamon Acropolis was probably ruined during the eartquake in 17 A.D.

Changes on the Borders of Bergama

Heroon

THE HEROON (IMPERIAL CULT)

The peristyle building seen on the left side while climbing up from the parking lot on the Acropolis, belongs to the Heroon. This building was dedicated to the cult of Pergamene kings who literally reached their gods after their deaths, during Hellenistic and Roman periods. Among these, especially Attalos 1 (241-197 B.C.) and Eumenes II (197-159 B.C.) were defied.

The building consisted of a courtyard, of a cult room and other rooms surrounding the courtyard. The courtyard could be reached passing through the two entrances at the west side and leading the way through the long corridors. Around the courtyard, there are thin marble columns. At the north of the courtyard, there was a hall which was separated by a group of pillars. This hall must have been used as an assembly room during the meal ceremonies of the cult. At the north of the hall, the cult room which had dimensions of 6x12 m. took place. On the north wall of this room there was a niche for a sculpture. Being restored during the Roman Empire period, the cult room in the building was styled as a square with dimensions of 12x13 m. A podium was constructed on the back wall and columns with conic capitals were placed over the walls. Thus cult room, like a tower, had the appearance of a two-storeyed building.

In the excavations undertaken in Heroon, no cemetery could have been found. During these excavations, beneath the Heroon, a leading building, resembling the Hellenistic period style, but more simple, and house

emnants belonging again to the same period were brought to light. These houses have
been partly uncovered.

Like the Heroon, all houses had their own
cisterns. Near the entrance of the Heroon,
at the north end of the northern passage, a
very big cistern was located. At the west side
of the Heroon, beneath the house which
was called "Cistern House", lots of canals,
cisterns and water channels were found.
This building probably belonged to the of-
ficers managing the water system of the city. As much as it was understood from the
writings explored during excavations, city
cisterns were supposed to be in working
condition all the time. Especially when the
city was subjected to a besiegement, the
water was supplied from these cisterns.

Opposite the Heroon, at the site of north-
west road, series of single-roomed shops
took place. The aim of building a gallery
above these shops, between the terrace of
Athena and its altar cannot be explained.

Heroon-Its Plan and Reconstruction

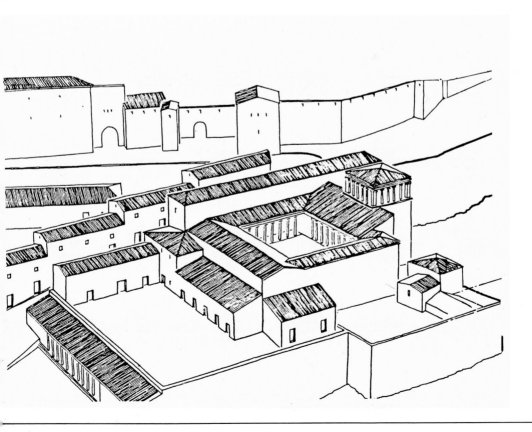

THE ALTAR OF ZEUS

The Altar of Zeus, built in the memory of the victory gained against the Galations during the period of Eumenes II (197-159 B.C.), was located in the middle of the area which is at the south of the Temple of Athena and 25 m. below it.

This terrace, having an entrance at the east, measured 69 by 77 metres. The entrance of the Altar is, however, at the west. The Altar had dimensions of 36.44x34.20 m., and it was constructed two-storeyed over the five-staired Krepidoma. The first floor of the building which was in the shape of a horseshoe, was massive. The outer side of this part was decorated with high relief plates which implied Gigontomakhia. These friezes surrounding the pedestal were 120 m. long and 2.30 m. high. The upper floor was surrounded by Ionic stoa. This floor was climbed up with the broad stairs at the west, and the rectangular space where the table-of-sacrifice was located, was reached. This rectangular table-of-sacrifice in the courtyard was surrounded with a wall which had a horseshoe shape. Inside and

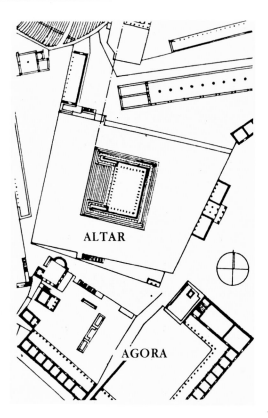

Plan of Zeus Altar.(Up)
Its Model (Down)

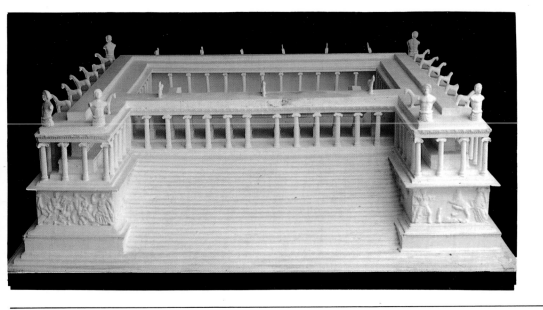

Frieze of Zeus Altar (Detail)

outside the wall, there were galleries decorated with ionic columns, but the galleries inside could not have been completed. Over a stone bank that surrounded the external galleries completely, there were, most probably, sculptures. On the inner side of the wall, there were low relief plates relating the life of Telephos, the legendary founder of Pergamon.

In the Altar, the sacrifices were slaughtered at the lower part then were taken to the upper part where they were burnt and given to god. The women were allowed only to the first part of this ceremony. The right to go up to the place where the bodies were burnt, belonged only to men.

Now, let us mention the reliefs in the Altar:

In order to reach the staired west face, one has to go round any of the two sides of the building. Meanwhile, the high relief friezes that took place on the pedestal can be seen. These high reliefs that were among the best examples of Bergama sculpture school, were in baroque style. Another important feature of these reliefs was that the names of the artists who made these figures were scraped on the upper borders.

On the entrance to the sacred area, at the east, first Zeus and Athena relief groups were seen. This face was, at the same time, the center of the frieze. Here, Zeus is shown fighting with three gigantes. Goddess Athena, with helmet on her head, a shield in her left hand and her medusa-headed Aigi (made of snake skin) on her breast, seizes the hair of a young gigant who is shown as winged and naked. (Gaia, the mother of the gigantes, begs Athena to forgive her son Akyoneus, but the snake of Athena has

A Detail from the Relief Group of Zeus and Athena (From Zeus Altar)

already poisoned the young gigant.) Nike is shown approaching to celebrate the victory and to crown Athena with a garland of laurel.

The eastward frieze: Leto, the mother of Artemis and Apollon, with the torch in her hands had burned the wings of bird-feeted gigant Tityos, and the gigant had fallen on his back.

Artemis and Apollon are shown fighting against the gigantes. In front of Apollon, the god of sun, lies the gigant Ephialtes whose eye had been wounded by Apollon. At the end of the face, Ares is shown passing with his chariot over the gigant he had knocked down.

At the north of the Altar of Zeus, gods concerning night and darkness were carved. in this part, besides Orion, the god of Stars, Nyx, the god of night and Moirae, goddesses of fate, Aphrodite took place, too. On the right end of the northward frieze, the chariot of Poseidon, god of sea was seen. On the west face, gods concerning sea were depicted.

Also, the struggles of Triton, god of waves, Poseidon's wife Amphitrite, Amphitrite's father Nereus and his wife Doris with the Gigantes were depicted. The one who was carved with a beard and overall and who was rushing the stairs might be god Hephoistos.

On the left inner side of the Altar stairs, a gigant figure trying to protect himself from the torch of Nymphe took place.

On the right-west frieze, the Dionysus group was depicted. On the frieze at the south of the altar there was the description of the war between the gods of light and day and the Gigantes. Helios, god of sun, Selenos, Eos, Zeus' mother Rheia took place in this part. On the internal walls of the second floor of the Altar, there were low relief plates which related the life of Telephos, the legendary founder of Pergamon. The plates had the sizes of 1.58x0.70 m.

The incidents related on the plates were such:

Auge, the daughter of the Arcadian king Aleos, gave birth to a child as a result of her secret relation with Herakles. Thereupon the king putting his daughter in a large box

Details from the Altar Friezes

Details from the Altar Friezes

The Remainders of the foundation of Zeus Altar

left her in sea and took her child to a mountain. The box came to the shores of Pergamon and was taken to the Mysian King Teuthros. Since the king had no child of his own, he adopted Auge. Meanwhile, the illegitimate child, given suck by a lion, was found under a plane-tree by his father Herakles.

Coming to Tenthonia, Telephos helped the king who had been fighting with his enemies. The king, therefore, wanted him to marry his exdaughter (?) Auge. But a snake which springed between Auge and Telephos prevented the wedding. The scenes following this one are: mother's recognizing her son, the death of Teuthras, Telephos' becoming king and his marriage to Hiera.

Following these scenes, Telephos' taking part in Trojan wars was described. During these wars, Achilles injured him with his spear. His injury was not healed. There was a soothsayer who had said that the only one who could heal the injury was the one who had done it. Thus, Telephos went to Achilles! country. In Argos, he captured the youngest son of Agamemnon, Orestes, in order to force him in making an ointment for his injury. At the last plate, Telephos is shown lying in a bed.

Some architectural pieces which were found in the Altar, during the excavations done between 1878-1890, in the temple of Zeus, were later taken to Berlin. Today, these pieces are exhibited in the Berlin Museum.

Upper Agora

THE UPPER AGORA

To the south of the altar of Zeus, a terrace downwards, the Upper Agora was located. Agora which was conformed to the condition of the land, has an L-shape, with a size of 83.7 m. to 43.5 m. The north-east, east, south-west and south sides of Agora are surrounded by Doric style galleries. Behind these galleries, there are narrow stores. Because of the slope of the land the southern gallery was built doublex and in "Hanging construction style" Thus the slope was prevented.

The lower flat rooms were used as ware houses. In the Upper Agora, all the constructions belong to the Hellenistic Age, except the one with apsides, which is located in the north-west corner of the Agora. This construction was renewed during the Roman Age.

In the west of Agora, there is a temple in Prostylos style, with a size of 12.30 m. to 6.70 m. It has antelis in Doric and Ionic style. The temple which was constructed in 2nd century B.C., was perhaps built in the honour of the god of merchants, Hermes. In front of the temple there is an altar. The meaning of an older building, which resembles the temple in the northern corner of the West gallery, has not been explained yet. The Agora which had a stone floor (0,40 m. to 0,60 m.) kept its original style until the Middle Ages, without having any restorations. In 8th century, the stones that were taken from the foundation of Particuses, were used in the construction of the Byzantian defense walls.

THE ATHENA TEMPLE AND STOA

Athena Temple - Reconstruction of Propylon

In Acropolis, at the left side of the entrance of the upper gate, there was a Holy Place, with a temple dedicated to the town goddess, Athena. Now, only the foundations of the temple can be visited. The temple which was constructed in 4th century B.C. is known as the oldest temple of Pergamon. It has a Doric style and a plan of 6x10 column peripteros. It is situated on a two-staired krepidoma with a size of 12,72 m. to 21,77 m. The temple the cella of which is divided into two parts must have been dedicated to Zeus, as well as Athena.

The foundations of the temple were joined with iron and wooden clamps. The clamp traces are now apparent. The temple was constructed by using local andezit stones. The stoa was made in 2nd B.C. to the memory of the victory gained against Galats. But we understand from some ruins that there were some restorations before that period. The sharp side of the south part of the land was supported by a wall of engraved stones. In the western side, the upper side of the theatre was also surrounded by a high wall. There is a passage of 29 stairs at the beginning of this wall, which can be the way to the theatre. It can be said that this passage was built to enable the passing in smaller groups.

The entrance to the Holy Place has andezit floors. Propylon was constructed in doublex style; in the lower flat there are four columns in Doric style, whereas in the higher flat, the four columns were built in Ionic style. In the Arkhitreas between these two flats the writing states: "From King Eumenes to the victory giving Athena". In the balcony of the second flat, the armours of the defeated Galats are carved. The original restored pieces of the Propylon are now displayed in the Berlin Pergamon Museum. Through Propylon, we pass into the two-floored Stoa. The Stoa is situated in the north-south and east-west directions. The north-south gallery is 40 meters in length and 5,47 meters in width. In the lower flat there are 17 Doric columns. The east-west gallery is 65 meters in length and its width is two times longer than the width of the other gallery. The entrance to both of the galleries are made by two staircases. In the backward walls of the gallery, there are niches in where statues were displayed. In these niches, the works of the artists, such as Epigonos, Phyromachios, Stratonikos and Antigonos, were found. The second flat of the gallery was a speciality of the Pergamon architecture. As a result, the empty foundation was built in Doric-Ionic style. The in-

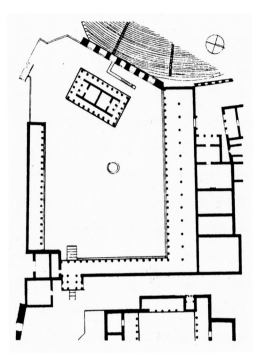

side of the backward walls of the gallery were covered by marble plates of 1.80 meter height. Between the Ionic columns of the higher flat galleries, there were 42 "Scarecrow" plates of 1.13 meter height. On the sides of these marble "Scare-crow" plates, looking to the Holy Place, there were reliefs showing the armours of the defeated Galats.

In the Athenian Holy place, there were art collections of Pergamon kings and booties gained in the victory over Galats. Groups of bronze statues were displayed on a marble base in the middle of the Holy Place. This "Base" was renewed during the Roman Age. In this age, a statue of Emperor Augustus (31 B.C. - 14 A.D.) was displayed here.

The Plan of Athena Temple and the Sacred Square (up) and their remainders (down)

Sacred Stoa and Library

THE PERGAMON LIBRARY

The library was situated behind the north Stoa in the Holy Place. It was constructed by the order of King Eumenes II. The entrance to the western rooms of the library was done through the lower flat of the north Stoa. There was a room of 12 meters height and 3 meters width. From there, passing through a narrow and small hall three little rooms could be reached. Of these rooms, the one that had normal sizes was on the eastern side. Passage to this room was done through the second flat of Stoa. This room was consisted of 4 halls related to each other. The largest room had a size of 16 to 13 m. and was probably used as a reading room. The room was on the eastern side and had stone podiums on its walls. These podiums, as well as the clamp holes that

were used to pin the book-shelves to the walls, can be seen also today.

The books were placed on the northern and western sides due to dampness on the south and west sides. There were also empty spaces of 0,50 m. between the walls and the book-shelves. There was a statue of Athena Porthenos over the base in the middle of the north wall. This statue was a smaller copy of the statue of Phidias which had been dedicated to Parthenon, in the Athena Acropolis in the Classical age. According to the ancient resources, there used to be 200.000 written documents in Pergamon library. These documents were kept in other buildings, towards the northern side. Eumenes II tried very hard for the library having a worth of worldly degree. The king made the artists and scientists come to Pergamon. Thus, Pergamon became a science and art center. As we learn from Strabon, Neleus hid the books of Aristoteles and Teophrostos. These books were searched both by Pergamon and Alepandia. At last,

Pergamon possessed them by giving gold as much as their weight to the heirs of Neleus. Thus Egypt restricted the export of papyrus to Pergamon. papyrus, at that time, was the easiest material used for writing. Thus this restriction made life hard for Pergamon writers. The Sardesian artist, Krates, prepared the first examples of goat (skin) on which writings could be made. This paper which was made of goat leather (skin) was named, after Pergamon, as "Pegiminae Chartae". This name, after some variations turned into "Parchment". Parchment was more useful and lasting than papyrus. In the challenge between papyrus and parchment made in Rome, parchment came first because of its properties.

By using parchment, the works of the Classical Age were written down and increased in number. In Pergamon this number reached to 200.000. In the library, there were precious stones such as the statue of Athena Porthenos, the bronze statue of poet Homeros, the bust of the woman poet Sapho, as well.

In 47 B.C., the library of (Alexandria) was burned during a war. In 41 B.C., it was moved to Alexandria and was given as a present to Cleopatra by Antonius. After that all books were burned down in a fire in Alexandria. Although its library had been moved to Alexandria, Pergamon kept its place, up to the end of Ancient Age, as a science and education center.

Sacred Stoa and Library

THE PALACES OF THE KINGS

To the east of the Attonion Holy place, just beside the eastern wall of Acropolis, there were palaces of the Pergamon kings and secondary degree buildings related to them. Palaces were without ornamentation and were 40x50 square meters in size. They had peristyle plan home types. Rooms were built around a courtyard which had columns. Although no documents were found, in archaeological excavations, about the successive owners of these palaces, it was found out that they were in possession of Pergamon Dynasty. The group of buildings in the outmost north belonged to the founder of the Pergamon kingdom, Philetairos (281-263 B.C.).

This group of buildings were then changed to barracks in which the soldiers of the castle used to live. In the highest place of Acropolis, there was a fire tower. There is a vagueness in the excavation traces found on the rocks on the north of this tower. It is not certain whether these traces belong whether to the oldest Zeus Holy Place or to the sight tower of the 1st and 2nd palaces.

It is highly probable that here is the place of the water tower which was at the center of ancient Pergamon. The rounded, huge cistern nearby was built to keep extra water. (This cistern is known by the visitors as the ''Wishing-well'', since there is a column in the middle where people throw money and wish for anything) The building groups towards the south belonged to Attalos I (241-197 B.C.), Eumenos II (197-159 B.C.), and Atalos II (159-138 B.C.), respectively. The stones that were used in the construction of the biggest palace in the south had the same characteristics as the stones excavated from the great altar. It is therefore concluded that this palace dates to 160 B.C., to the time of Eumenes II. In the north-east corner of the palace, there was an altar with mosaic floors. In the north-western room, there was a mosaic fresque. This mosaic is important, in the sense that, it is signed by Xephaistion. There were also two cisterns belonging to the palaces. Among the two, the one belonging to the big building can be seen in the west side of the ruins, along the road. This palace had an ornamental entrance.

There is also a probability that the remaining foundations of the Palaces of the Kings can be traced towards the area of Traian Temple which was constructed in later periods

Architectural Plan of the King Palaces

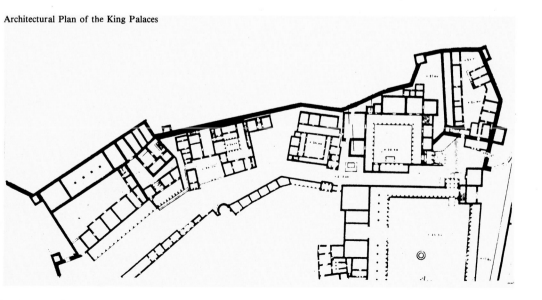

Remainders of the King Palaces

THE CANALS – THE AQUEDUCTS

The canals of the ancient Pergamon can be seen by looking down from the northern corner of Arsenal towards the hills in the northern direction. The Aqueducts seen from there, must have been constructed in the Roman Age. The researches made in this subject proved that the water necessary for the Pergamon Acropolis was taken from earthenware water pipes in the Hellenistic Age, and from water arcades in the Roman Age.

The oldest canal known in Bergama in the Attalos canal. This canal was made of earthenware water pipes, in a single line, which passed from the northern sides of Selinus valley and from the western sides of Çaputlu hills, and ended in the Gymnasium area.

Demophon water way is constructed out of double clay pipes. That water way, just like the Attalos water canals, pass through the same slopes and close to Demophon and reach the fountain of streams.
Madradağ water system was constructed in the second century B.C. Each water system consisted of 240.000 clay pipes of 50-75 cm. length, which connected the water fountains of Madradağ to the water reservoir on the southern slopes of Soğucak Hill (hagios-georgios).

The water system reached the Pergamon castle by means of underground lead pipes passing over three valleys and two low hills. The lead pipes were extended through large holes in the ground and fixed there. The high pressured water pipes, (up to 20 Atu), may be observed as a collapsed line extending through the landscape. It is quite possible that the cisterns, fountains and houses of the castle received their water supply from a central water reservoir and distributed by clay pipes. The water system, that had been in use until the 3rd. century A.D., was destroyed by an earthquake in the year 262 A.D.

The population of the city · increased under the Roman reign. The water need of the area was supplied from the Kozak mountains. The waterway extended for 80 km. through the northern slopes of Soma-Bakırçay valley and carried into the city over archways.

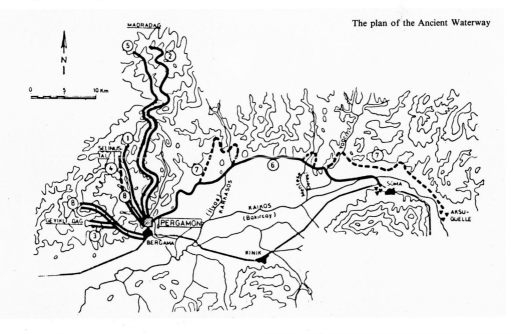

The plan of the Ancient Waterway

Cistern (up) and Ancient waterways (down)

Arsenal and Military Magazines

ARSENAL (MILITARY MAGAZINES)

In the northern side of Acropolis, there were five rectangular magazines. These magazines were constructed in the 3rd and 2nd centuries B.C. In these buildings, especially cereals and other friable things were kept. The bases were made up of walls close to each other, in the form of grate, to carry the weight upstairs. In order to secure a good air circulation, there were many holes dug in the walls. The original magazines were big and had wooden galleries that had roofs covered with tiles.

In those magazines, food, the soldier's armours and war equipments were kept.

In the excavations made in Arsenal, 800 shots which were made of 13 different diametered andezits, were found. These shots were thrown by slings in the form of catapults. They were stocked outside the magazines in the Ancient age. All shots were found in the lower Agora, in the place with wire gauze. The smallest of these andezit shots was of 15 cm. in diameter and weighed 2.8 kilograms.

Bergama Arsenal is the oldest armour and equipment depot. Such depots were generally set up in the headquarters of the legions during the Roman Age. At the southeast of the arsenal there was a barrack of king's troops. The northern-east wall of the barracks is the most carefully preserved ruin of the Hellenistic Age.

THE TRAIAN TEMPLE

The Traian Temple stands on a 60 to 70 metre terrace, to the north of the Athena Sacred area. This temple was built for the Roman Emperor Traian (98-117) and was completed by Emperor Handrianus (117-138) who reigned after his death. Because of the sloping land, the terrace was fit on the strong vaults and retaining walls, half size, facing southwest. The ruins of the houses of Hellenistic Age was found under the vaults of Traianeum. And on the east of the temple beneath the surface of the region, buildings belonging to Hellenistic Age, were dug out. They were possibly the extensions of the king's palaces towards west.

The temple set on a high podium with 6x10 coloumns, was built according to the a peripteros plan. The building, in the Korith pattern, is 18 metres high. Temple is surrounded by galleries with coloumns on three sides. No gallery was built in front of the temple so that it can be seen easily from the city below. The gallery behind stood on higher terrace in comparison with the side galleries. This gives a good background behind the temple. There are two bases, on the two sides of the temple, near the back wall of the area. The one in the shape of a semi-circle belongs to the period of Attalos II. The semi-circle shaped sitting bank of the exedra is connected with the base of statue in that one. This base is at the Berlin Pergamon Museum today. The other base with the form of quadrangel belongs to the Roman Age. This base was rebuilt by using Hellenistic pieces in the Roman period. To-day only the foundations of the both monuments are seen on the area.

The head and other pieces, belonging to the kolossal statues of Emperor Traian and Hadrias are exposed in the excavation, done in Traian Sacred area, This indicates that this area is dedicated to both emperors.

The Armored Torso from the Traian Temple Remainders. (it is supposed to be belonged to Emperor Hadrianus) (up) The Restorations of the Traian Temple by the German Archeological Institute (down)

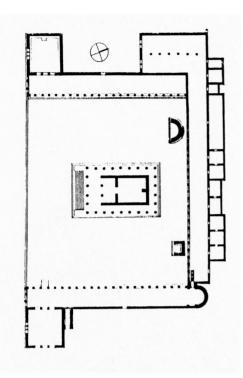

The restoration work is being carried out by the German Archeological Institude.During the restoration work which has been carried out until now, the foundation of the front part of the vaults are renewed and reinforced by the circuit-wall. The northeast terrace and the most of the upper gallery coloumns with their arkhitreos were erected upright. Having the walls reinforced in the southeast and northwest, some coloumns were erected.

The restoration work of the Sacred Area is carried out by using recent technology and it is earthquake resistant.

The temple's west-end room floor and the south wall was restored again.So Dionysos Temple and Theatre are let to be watch from above by the visitors.

The Plan of Traian Temple (up)
General View of Traian Temple (down)

A view from Traian Temple (right)

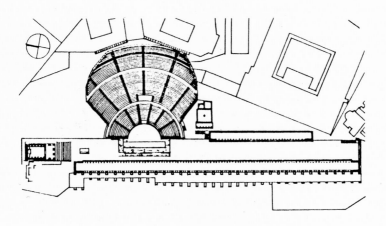

Architectural Plan of Acropolis Theater and its Terrace

THEATRE AND THEATRE TERRACE

Looking from the restored western room of the Traian sacred area down to the south, the Bergama Theatre, one of the most upright theatres of the antique age is seen. This theatre which was built in the Hellenistic Age, was erected fitting the steep slope land. The theatre with the capacity of 10000 spectators was divided into three parts by two diazomas. The steps are situated from upstairs to downstairs in the form of a dagger. And there are eighty sitting rows. All of the sitting rows were made of andesit except the marble honour box below. The stage was set up at the theatre terrace over the strong wooden hatıl only during the ceremony games in Hellenistic Age. This section consists of a low stage where the play used to be presented and the scaenfrons in the background. Because the stage blocks the Dionysos Temple which lies in the north of theatre terrace. So it was fixed only when the play would be presented. The wooden stage in front of the place of the theatre orchestra, keeps its good form. These holes were recovered by stone blocks after the plays. A stone podium was built in front of the theatre in the Roman Period. That is the area which is seen today. After having built a new theatre in the city below, this podium was used as a dressing bleacher. The wall which has high arched niches in the upper part of the theatre was built in the Roman Period. There is a terrace of about 250 metres long in front of the theatre.

There are galleries, made of andesit stones in the east and west part of the terrace. In order to keep the high pressure within the theatre terrace, some substructures had to be built at some places. And the building at the row between the theatre and eastern gallery might be a gathering place for the players. In the north of the terrace stands the Dionysos Temple.

Remainders of Dionysos Temple

THE TEMPLE OF DIONYSOS

The Temple of Dionysos which is located on the North of the theatre terrace whose lenght is approximately 250 m., was also controlling the panorama of the terrace. The temple which was built up in the 2nd c. BC. rises on a podium. It was contructed in Ion style as a prostylos. The dimensions of its stylobat are 20.22x11.80 m. The temple is climbed by a 25 step stairs in front of it. The back of the temple, which was made of andesit in the Hellenistic Era, leans against stone. In the Roman Era, the temple was rebuilt from marble, according to its old plan. The parts, which are standing today, belong to the Roman Era. After a great fire in the 3 rd C. A.D., the temple was

reconstructed by Emperor Caracalla Emperor Caracalla was brought to Asklepio after he had a dangerous ship accident i Gallipoli. The Emperor has got better there in a short period, and he set up his statu on the sacred square of Asklepion, as thanksgiving. Afterwards he rebuilt th Dionysos Temple from Marble which wa fell down into the theatre terrace i Acropol.

The Marble Niche Acroters which are be ing exhibited in the Museum of Bergama, ar supposed to be the acroters of the Dionyso Temple before, and concluded that the were brought to Asklepion during th Tetrarch Period. Another interestin speciality of the Dionysos Temple i Acropol is the seams of the Attic Ion Col umn bases which are digged into th ground. Today, the visitors can see the pro file seams of these Attic Ion Column Base

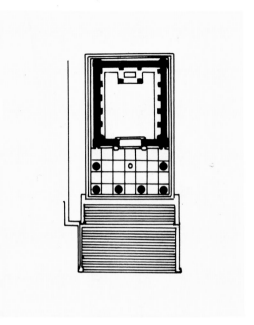

Plan of Dionysos Temple

Reconstruction of Dionysos Temple

THE SMALL GYMNASIUM (The Bath, Odeon, the Heroon)

It is coincised some building remains with vaults, on the way to the Archaic Road which is located on the South of the theatre terrace. Those remains, which were of a bath, are located on the South of the upper Agora and farther 100 m. from it towards South. They were found in the city excavations in 1973, which was started to be digged from the point of the upper castle between the sides of the city hill and the Upper Castle which is open to public today. The real room which is round; (tepidarium), is known by its large niche. From the other parts of the bath there are few remains which are left. The bath, with its mosaic decoration, is an early example of the Hellenistic Era. About 150 m. to the South, on the way to the Archaic Road, there is a complex building at left of the road, which

holds three parts that are connected with each other. It includes a bath on the western side, a lecture or concert hall (odeon) near to it, and the Cult hall on the Eastern side. The bath was built in the Roman Era. There is a narrow road which is located on the west of the bath. Beneath the road there stands a drainage canal. This canal leads to the canal which is under the main street. On the West-South of the extreme of the canal stands the remains of the general toilet (Latrine). This drainge canal was also used to clean the Latrine. Latrine was built up together with the bath. The entrance of the bath is located on the East side of the bath facing to the main street.

The columns which are located on the West of the yard are reset up by the assistance of the German Archeology Institute. Once there was a cistern on the top of the abscissa shaped cool water basin (frigidorium) which is located on the Northern part of the yard. Another cistern which is located on the Western direction of this still can be imagined in its old form with its water proff ground which is plastered with Horasan mortar and the narrow stairs leading up. In the South of the yard, there stands the hot bathing rooms (caldarium). The stokehole of this bathing places was also being used as a woodshed.

In the East, the bath yard has another passageway. The odeion also provides a connection door between the yard and Odeon on the top level of the sitting lines. And this proves us that, the young men in the gymnasium were also interested in musical education, as well as the sport games on the yard. There are three rooms and a corridor of stairs between the odeon and the stokehole of the bath. These rooms are supposed to be the kitchen and the pantry stores for the cult meals of heroon, by the diggers. Today, they are partly covered with a protective ceilign. The plan of the Odeon is in dagger form. In order to have a better usage from a limited place, the abscissa sitting steps, which give a passage way to the audience, are divided into two parts from above to downwards.

The "Marble Hall" which is located on the East of Odeon, belonging to a person from Bergama, is a cult place, a heroon. This person, who had done many charities during his life time, was respected as if a god. The portrait head of the cult statue, which is in the Museum of Bergama today, was found in front of the cult abscisse. This head is the portrait of Diodoros Pasparos from Bergama who was an influential person of the heroon cult in 70 B.C. In the excavations, was also found some reliefs. During the restoration of the "Marble Hall" the originals of these reliefs were replaced with their moulages, and are being exhibited in the Museum of Bergama, today. The method used on the subjects which are figured on these reliefs, such as a fighting cock, helmet, star helping the victory of Dioscures, sword, spear and armour; shows that they belong to a later period than the portrait of Diodoros Pasparos. They are likely to be the result of the restoration by Tiberius in 17 A.D., after an earthquake.

Ancient Road

FOOD HOUSE OIL AND WINE STORES

There were rooms of a simple storage house near the marble hall towards the east. This food house was composed of three rooms; one that had a furnace in the rocky ground which was on the left side of the road; one that had pictures over its walls and one that had a grate in it and which was partly constructed in rock. There was also a building remaining on the eastern side which was a store. There was a narrow entrance door near it. In the store, there were big earthenware jars in which oil or wine were kept.

Views from the Small Gymnasium Bath

Wine and Oil Shops (up)
The Marble Room (down)

City Excavation and Ancient Buildings (right)

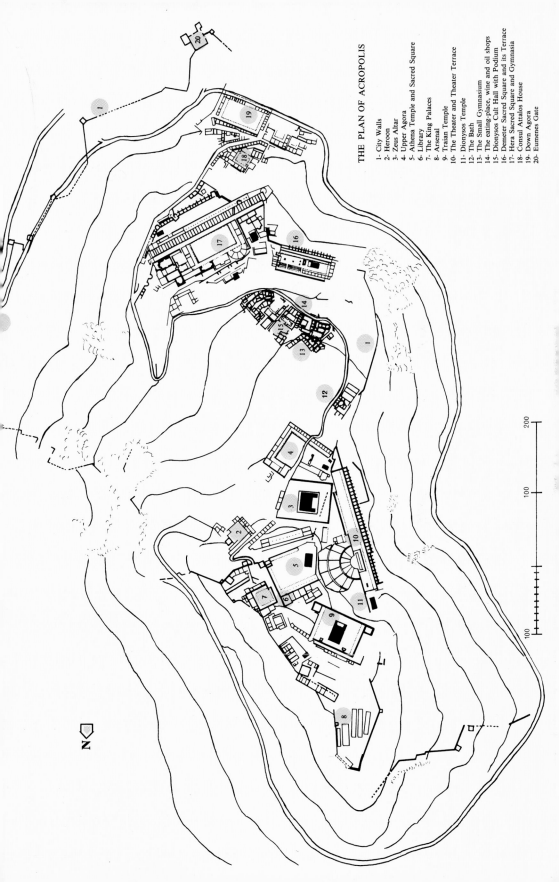

THE PLAN OF ACROPOLIS

1- City Walls
2- Heroon
3- Zeus Altar
4- Upper Agora
5- Athena Temple and Sacred Square
6- Library
7- The King Palaces
8- Arsenal
9- Traian Temple
10- The Theater and Theater Terrace
11- Dionysos Temple
12- The Bath
13- The Small Gymnasium
14- The eating-place, wine and oil shops
15- Dionysos Cult Hall with Podium
16- Demeter Sacred Square and its Terrace
17- Hera Sacred Square and Gymnasia
18- Consul Attalos House
19- Down Agora
20- Eumenes Gate

Remainders of Dionysos Cult and Podium

DIONYSOS CULT HALL WITH PODIUMS AND OTHER BUILDINGS

On the eastern side of the wine store, standing on the ancient road, there was a narrow street stretching forward to the north. On the western side of this narrow street, there was a terrace. This terrace was the front terrace of the hall dedicated to the cult of Dionysos. The hall had podiums and 24x10 m. dimensions.

There were small rooms on the left side of this front terrace. In the terrace there is a fountain remaining and a deep, big cellar in the tuff rocky place on the eastern side. One of the important characteristics of the hall was that the podiums that were 1 m high and 2 m. deep and which went through the walls.

On the podiums, the cult group used to eat their meals on the marbles of the front face. During the meals the people laid on the ground with their heads looking to the middle of the hall. That was a sign showing that Dionysos was greatly appreciated by his folk.

Opposite to the entrance of the cult hall, there was a cult niche and in front of it an altar. (This altar is displayed in the Bergama Museum) Over the altar there are reliefs about Dionysos cult.

Mounting the podiums was done by little stairs. All the hall walls were full of pictures. A few pictures remaining today were illustrating cult equipment designs. The hall was covered with a tiled roof but it was changed in time. The running fountain in the terrace and the deep cellar in the courtyard were also related to Dionysos cult.

Dionysos cult was greatly loved and appreciated by the ordinary people. The location of the wine stores which are near to the cult hall also enforces this idea.

Dionysos cult ceremonies were a means of gathering the merchants and artists to the podiumed hall during the religious rites.

Dionysos cult hall had a simple construction style and interior planning. This proves that the cult group was not very rich.

On the southern side of the podiumed hall, towards the right of the middle road, the ruins of a peristyle house can be seen. This house had a Turkish bath in it. The construction period of this house dates back to the Hellenistic Age. Some of the columns surrounding the courtyard were set up again after being restored. At the time of the Roman Empire, the house was enlarged and organized again. Moreover, a private Turkish bath and a big water depot were added to the house.

The Columned House and Byzantine Megalio.

On the south-eastern side of the peristyle house, along the ancient mainroad, there were stores and working rooms. Surely there were house rooms on the upper floors and behind these places. On the rocky cistern by the road, there was a big building with a stone arch, which might have been a public fountain.

During the town excavations which began in 1973, many ruins were excavated. One of these ruins was the big building remaining on the eastern side of the excavation area. There is a possibility that the place where this building was located, was a Holy Place during the Hellenistic ages. There was possibly the Bergama Megalesion of the great mother goddess of Anatolia, Kybele.

The large columned courtyard was surrounded with galleries from four sides. Behind the eastern gallery there was a cult and an adjacent room. During the period of the Roman Empire, a magnificient Exodia was placed on the northern gallery. Later, working places were moved inside and the galleries were divided into smaller rooms.

DEMETER HOLY PLACE AND ITS TERRACE

During the reign of Philetairos (281-263 B.C.), in Acropolis, there was the Demeter Holy Place outside the defence walls. However, some ruins that are excavated in later years, prove that Demeter dates back before the period of Philetairos.

In the holy place reserved for Demeter and her daughter Kore, the "asıltnak" over the rocky place remained in its own place, where as the terrace was many times enlarged towards the south. The cause of these enlargements was the slope of the land.

Philetairos and his brother Bumenes constructed a temple in memory of their mother, Boa. This temple was made of local andezit stones and was in megoran style. It was approximately 6,45 m. to 12,70 m. in size. Over the marble frieze in Arşit, between each girland hanger, there was a decorative ornamentation of a bull head

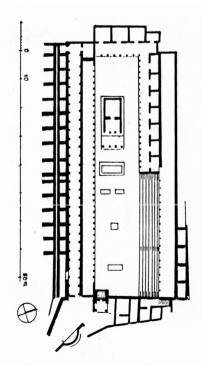

This Girland ornamentation was appreciated in the Hellenistic age, too, and in later years it became the main ornamentation figure of the Roman Period. There was an altar belonging to the Eastern Temple. This altar had a size of 7.00 m. to 2.30 m. Between the Propylon and main altar, there were also other little altars. This temple was changed during the Roman Age, to a Corinth style prostylos with marble columns.

There was a terrace of 43 m. length on the northern side of the castle. The construction of the northern border and of the altar started at the same period.

The enlargement of the gallery towards the north was done upon the order of Queen Apollonis (wife of Attalos II, 241-197

The Freize with Ox Head and Ghirland (up) Demeter Sacred Square Propylon (down)

Frieze with Demeter

B.C.). The queen also gave the order for the construction of the entrance door which had Aial headgears. The columns of the entrance door were set up again in time.

The front courtyard of the temple which had 43 m. length and 20 m. width was built in the shape of a theatre, on the northern side. The people taking place in Mysters ceremonies used to sit on the ten-staired benches.

Construction of the other rooms in Holy Place was also financed by the Queen. A queen's donation meant that this holy place was given great importance by the Pergamon women. There, in certain nights, the goddess' festivals were celebrated under the beams of the torches.

Once in a year, in October, there were Tesmophoria festivals celebrated in honour of Demeter and the wife of the god of the underworld, Persephone. Only married women were allowed to join these festivals. A relief showing this ritual is being displayed in the Bergama Museum, at present. In this marble relief plate, Demeter was pictured with her torch in her hand near the altar. There was a wellon the left stone and it had a shape that did not strike the eye. It was a votive offering well. Women visiting the Holy Place were to leave their presents for Demeter and her daughter Persephone to this place. (The presents were pigs, cookies etc.)

7- Demeter had a daughter, named Persephone. Once, while she was collecting flowers with her friends, she was captured by the God of Underworld, Hades. Demeter became very sorry for losing her daughter and so she took all her presents back from the earth. That year, nothing grew on earth. Demeter would never give anything to earth until she saw her daughter. So God Zeus ordered his brother Hades to send Persephone back to the world. Hades, claiming that Persephano would come back, sent her to the world, to Demeter's place. According to the contract, every year, for four months Persephone would stay in the underworld, and during the other 8 months she would stay by her mother on earth.

Taking her daughter back, Demeter gave fertility back to the earth. She taught to a man called Triptolen in Eleusis, how to plant crops. She also told him the things that ought to be done during the mysterious ceremonies. People joining the ceremonies should not say anything about them and thus live in happiness...

When Persephone came to earth, the soil began to freshen, spring came and the flowers started to flourish everywhere. When she returned back to underworld everywhere withered up.

Remainders of Hera Sacred Square

HERA HOLY PLACE AND GYMNASIUMS

On the narrow terrace over the upper Gymnasium, there was the Holy Place of Hera, wife of the father of gods, Zeus. This place was consisted of a temple that was surrounded by a rounded Exodra on the west and by a columned gallery on the east. The temple which was mounted by a many staired open ladder, carried almost the same characteristics with a Roman podiumed temple. It was a prostylos in Doric style.

According to the votive offering inscription it was constructed by Attolos II (159-138 B.C.). In the cellar of the temple, archaeologists found a huge statue of a man (Istanbul Archaeological Museum). It might be Zeus' cult stone (because then, people used to worship both Hera and Zeus, there) or it might be the statue of Attalos II. This question has not been answered yet.

On the southern side of the Hera Holy Place, downwards, there was a Gymnasium. The ruins visited today are the remaining parts of a building complex that was built to serve for the education and sporting of young people at the time of Kingdom.

The gymnasium which was built during the kingdom period was enlarged in Roman

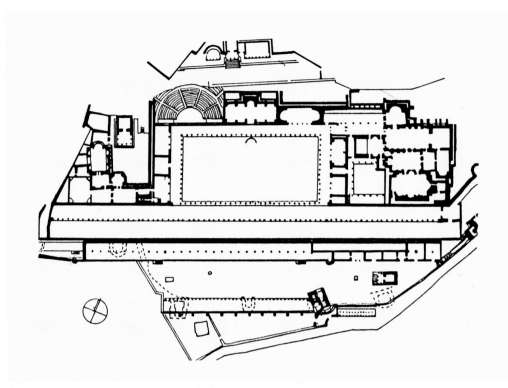

The Plan of Hera Holy Place and Gymnasium (up)

Reconstruction of Gymnasium

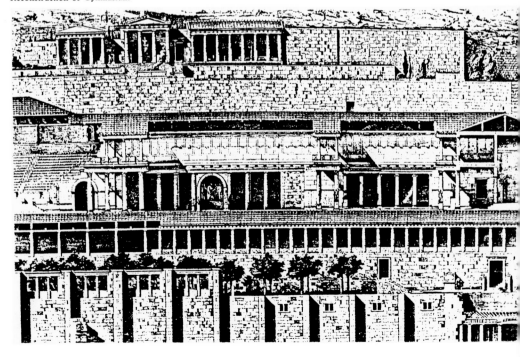

Ages. From the ruins, this change can clearly be seen in the terrace of the upper Gymnasium. In the upper terrace, on the western side of the Gymnasium courtyard, there was a little temple belonging to the Hellenistic age. This temple was constructed at the beginning of 2nd century B.C., but was changed later in the same century. It was understood from the colossal statue found during the excavations of the temple that this temple was dedicated to Asklepiós. The Gymnasium was a complex surrounded by buildings that were placed around a large courtyard which also was surrounded on four sides by pillared galleries.

The courtyard was limited by two Turkish baths on eastern and western sides.

On the western side of the pillarred courtyard, in the middle, there were the sportsmen's basins in which they used to bath after the races. In the north-eastern corner, there was a conference hall which resembles a closed theatre. This hall had a capacity of 1000 people. The place in the middle of the northern side was the main room of the Gymnasium. There was another room with two apsides adjacent to this main room on the eastern side. From the inscriptions it is understood that this hall was the private hall of the Emperor.

Remainders of Gymnasium

The decoration of these rooms and the upper floor was made quite magnificiently.

On the wall coverings, pillars and fringes, a kind of different marble, brought from distant regions, was used. The Turkish bath walls, on the east, were covered with the same kind of marble plates.

With the ruins of the Turkish bath which were kept in good order till our time, the ancient locations can clearly be visualized. The bath on the east had a central heating system.

On the southern side of the Gymnasium, the sloping land was effectively used to construct a long running field and a closed Stadium building.

In the stadium, there was also the southern gallery of the upper courtyard. The closed stadium was lightened through the narrow windows on the south wall. But later, in the Hellenistic period, because of the danger of collapsing, the south was also closed.

Pergamon Gymnasiums were the greatest profane building complexes of the town. The complex, with all its main features and location, was Hellenistic. At Roman times, many changes were made, especially on the largest terrace on the top. But, the lower and middle terraces kept their conditions in Hellenistic period, at the time of Eumenes II (197-159 B.C.), as well. This building was constructed on three terraces which enlarge one by one as it goes up.

On the lower terrace, there was the children's gymnasium, on the middle terrace the youngs' was located, and on the upper terrace, there was the adult's gymnasium. Through an arched open stairway, the staired passage of the middle gymnasium was reached. It was of a different architectural style which made use of two vaults crossing each other at a right angle. The middle Gymnasium was consisted of a long running field. On the eastern side, the foundations of a small temple were excavated. This temple was behind the large stairs and was constructed in the Hellenistic age. It was an anteli Prostylos one built in Corinth style. Ruins of the alter, in front of the temple were found during the excavations. On the opposite of the north altar, there was a building with two Doric pillars in front,

A Bath Tepidarium (up)
Hypokaust (down)

A Bath Calldarium (down)

which served the cult of the gods. From the inscriptions, it was understood that Hermes and Herakles which symbolize body power and speed, were worshipped. On the temple walls, the lists of successful Ephebosians were carved.

On the eastern side of the staired entrance of the middle gymnasium, there was a town fountain which was rectangular in shape and which had a roof constructed on a one column row. On the interior face of the front banister of the fountain, there were friction traces of the capes used for getting water. These traces can still be seen. On the western side of the staired entrance, the simple entrance of the children's Gymnasium was located. At present, there are very few remainings from the children's Gymnasium main walls. The backward wall was full of niches and honour projections. Moreover, there were many inscriptions carved on this wall which gave a list of the race winners.

Gymnasium-Race Road
A view from the Gymnasium.

Remainders of Consul Attalos' House

CONSUL ATTALOS' HOUSE

On the northern side of the lower Agora, over the high terrace, a house belonging to the Hellenistic age was excavated. This house which was restorated in Roman times (2nd century A.D.), belonged to a noble person, and was constructed around a columned Peristyle courtyard. The southern side of the house was ruined at the very early periods. The columned galleries of the countyard had two floors. The lower flat was of Doric style and was made of andezit stones. The upper flat carried Ionic highlights and was mad of marble. On the west, the largest room of the house, the assembly or feasting room of men (Oikos) was located. On the right side of the entrance, there was a Herme. In ancient times, it was used to carry the bronze head portrait of the host Attaloş. In the inscription, his name was clearly stated. He and his visitors were called to live prosperously. On the right side, there was a small cult room. In the bedrooms and sitting rooms, some precious wall pictures and base mosaics were found. These rooms were located on the northern side of the courtyard. Some of the mosaics belonged to the Hellenistic age. The wall pictures were from the time of the Roman Empire.

In the courtyard. There were three cisterns; a small Hellenistic cistern and two large Roman cisterns. A water pipe ran from the big cistern downwards to the fountain in Agora.

Down Agora

THE LOWER AGORA
(Market place)

The lower Agora was founded during the enlargement period in Pergamon, at the time of King Eumenes II, at the beginning of the 2nd century B.C. The Agora had 36x63 m. dimensions. It was surrounded by columned galleries on four sides. The Galleries were Doric in style and were doublex. Between the columns there were one roomed stores opening to the galleries.

Since the southern gallery was constructed on the slope of a hill, it had a lower flat. Thus, the northern gallery had the upper flat. The upper flat stores of the northern gallery were opening to the mainroad. On the left side of the road, mounting to Gymnasiums and on the lower part of Attalos' house, there were stores in various sizes. The inscriptions that were set up in the market place were important, in the sense that, the laws stated on them gave informations about the social life in town. There were also detailed kingdom rules about the construction of roads and houses, cleaning of canals and cisterns, etc. These subjects were among the duties of the town police. (Astynom inscription. Bergama

Museum) There was a well in the middle of the market place.

Ruins of houses were found during the excavations done in a triangular area, at the northwest direction of the Agora. In the lower Agora which had lost its importance in the 4th century A.D., a church was excavated. Also, ruins from Byzantine period were found. The part of Agora which was separated with a fence and which was covered with a protective roof, was used to protect the shots taken from the Arsenal at the north Acropolis, and the other works of that period.

The Plan of Down Agora and Eumenes Gate

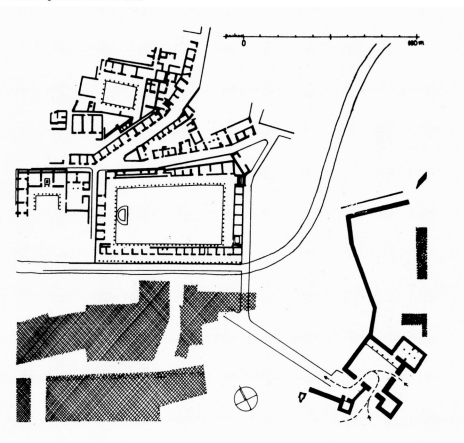

EUMENES DOOR

Upon the order of the most powerful king of Pergamon, Eumenes II (197-159 B.C.), the city walls were enlarged up to the southest border of Acropolis. The most eminent feature of the city; the city door was then founded here. The road coming from the valley passed through the precipice, turned left by making a narrow crossing on the strengthened door court and reached to the lower Agora which was on a higher level.

The striking appearance of the courtyard door was faded away with the pillarred gallery on the east wall. The door was protected with three towers, against the attacks from all sides. In times of peace, clerks exchanged money and lawyers performed their usual professions inside the city walls.

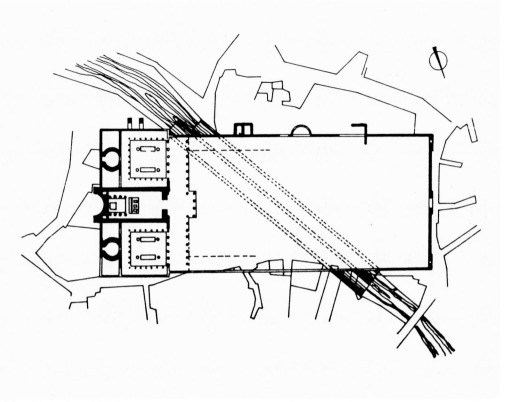

The Plan of Serapeion and its Channels

SERAPEION (THE TEMPLE OF EGYPTIAN GODS)

This temple which was most probably founded in the 2nd century A.D., during the time of emperor Hadrian (117-138), is in Bergama. At present, because of its red-bricked walls, it is called as the "Red Court" among people. This temple which is known as the greatest temple founded in Anatolia during Roman times, was located on an area of almost 260x100 m., and had almost 60x26 m. dimensions, The brick walls of the temple were almost 19 meters high. The temenos wall which was near the ancient bridge on Selinus on west, was left

nearly at 13 square meters. The temenos area on which the temple was located, was not dug out completely; only the eastern part of temenos was cleared of houses during the excavations.

The building complex in which the temple was included, was located on the eastern part of the temenos area. This building complex was consisted of a rectangularly-planned monumental building and two tower-like round buildings, added to both sides. The round buildings had 15 m. diameters and were 19 m. high. On the two sides of the temple, in front of the tower-like buildings, there were peristyled court-yards, surrounded with pillared galleries. Previously, in these courtyards, there were pools covered with onyl and wells of 3 m. depth near the pools. The roof of the galleries was carried by caryatids (columns in human form.) These were marble statues

Red Palace, Tower (up)
A Cariatid (down)

of a man and a woman leaning on each other's back, and were of Egyptian style. In front of the temple, along the entire width of the temenos area, there was a front courtyard surrounded with pillars. Behind this yard, come the door of the temple along the entire width of the temenos area, there was a front courtyard surrounded with pillars.

Behind this yard, come the door of the temple with 7 m. width and 14 m. height. The interior floor of the building was of marble. In the middle of that a podium of 1.50 m. height was located. On the step on the podium, there was, previously, a cult statue. The priest could go into this statue through an underground way and a hole in the middle of the stone, and could make his speech inside, and make the people believe that the gods were speaking.

In the temple, there was a gallery built on marble pillars. Since there was no window at the back, it stayed in half dark. In this part, there were entrances of two stairs which lead to the gallery and to the roof. The shape of the roof is not known. On the back wall of the temple, there was an outward apsis, but the reason of making this apsis is not known yet.

Since the Selinus spring passed through the temenos area, double tunnels with 9 m. width and 200 m. length were built over the spring. These tunnels are in a very good condition today. As a result of the temple's being constructed over a river, the Egyptian statues which are excavated, and the pools which were common for eastern culture, it can be concluded that this building was made for Egyptian gods. The temple must have been devoted to God Sespis with Iris, and Harpok rates worshipped in sowehere in Roman Empire. At Byzantine period, a church was founded in the "Red Court".

Today the walls of this church still stand in the main building. The excavations and researches in Serapeion still continue.

Interior Yard-Square, Pool and Cariatids (up)
A View from Serapeion (down)

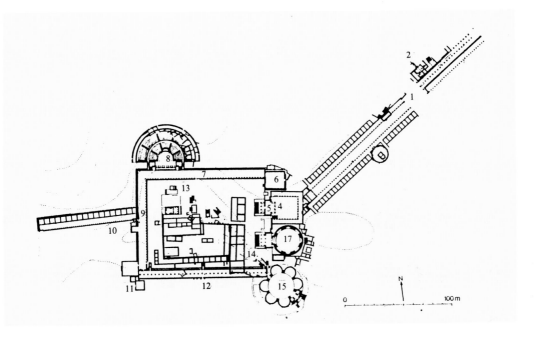

The Plan of Asklepion Holy Place:
1-Holy Road (Via Tecta) 2-The Fountain 3-The Mausoleum 4-5-Propylon 6-Library 7-The Northern Gallery 8-Theater 9-The Western Gallery 10-Hellenistic Stoa 11-Latrine 12-The Southern Gallery 13-Pool 14-Cryptoporticos 15-The Round Building 16-Peristyle House 17-Zeus Asclepios Temple.

ASKLEPION

Asklepion is to the west of Bergamon, outside the city. The Sacred Area in Epıdouros in Greece was brought to Pergamon in the 4th century BC and a health center was founded in that century. 18 constructure periods belonging to the Pre-Roman time were exposed in the excavation of Asklepion. From the beginning of the process, the Sacred Aera was widened and became the most famous health center of the period. The ruins that remain today belong to the constructions and changes that were carried out by Emperor Hadrianus (117-138 BC) In Bergamon, at that period patients were cured by soothing, sun bathing and by using some very special natural drugs. Death was forbidden in The Sacred Area since the only aim was to cure the patient. The writing upon the many entrance states the Law "Death is not allowed" Severe patients were taken out of the city and pregnant woman were not allowed to give birth inside. The patients coming for treatment were examined at the Main gate and were not let in if there were no treatment for their illnesses. Pausanian writes that the people spending last day of their lives were not let in and if they happen to get sick inside, they were taken out immediately.

Holy Road (Via Tecta) (up)
Remainders of Asklepion Propylon (down)

The entrance of Asklepion was through the big Virankapı, the very famous gate which is located in the area where Stadium and Amphitheatre also are located After the entrance through Virankapı, lies a sacred road (Via Tecta) about 820 m. long and 18.4 m. wide. This sacred road was covered with arches which fit on bases and columns, made of stone blocks. The Sacred road is floored by smoothly cut andesit stones and there is a canal which divides the road into two.

Before reaching Propylon there is a big fountain built in later times, in the north of the columned road. To the south of the fountain ruins of round grave mounments belonging to the time of Augustus (27 BC-14 AD) can be found. The Sacred Road extends s far as Propylon which was built by Claudius Charax, in mids of 2nd century B.C.

The foundations of Propylon, 4 to 12 meters in dimension can be seen from the western part of the columned road. Pieces of Propylon that have remained up to our day can be seen along the marble road.

Acroter (up)
The Snake-figured Column (down)

At present Akroter figures of Propylon are displayed in the Bergama museum. On the left side of this structure, there is the library which was the most important education center in the Empire.

The floor design of the library resembles a carpet with geometrical designs. Blue, white, green and light green marbles decorating the floor are in shapes of squares, triangles and circles. The large room is 16.5 18.5 m. The walls werebuilt in peristasis system to avoid humidity. During the excavations Emperor Hadrianus' statue was exposed in this library. This statue is displayed in Bergama Museum at present. At the base of the statue it was written that this statue was given as a present to the Emperor by Flavia Melitine. In smoll holes on the walls some parchment documents are also found. Pergamon Asklepion is the only

Asklepion Library (up)
A General View of Asklepion (down)

Asklepion with a library inside. Reading and resting rooms for the patients are also special to this Asklepion.

The courtyard of the Sacred Area in Asklepion is surrounded by galleries on three sides, north, west and south. The northern gallery is 128 m. to 8.5 m. in dimension.

In order to gain more space, the rear block wall is leaned to the dressed stone. The 70 cm space left between the retaining wall holding the higher layer and the second wall which is 82 cm. thick are first examples of a double-wall system Almost half of the 45 marble columns of this gallery are exposed.

Apart from the 10 columns that were constructed in brinth style, on the east edge of the northern gallery, remaining columns all have Ionian highlights. These brinth columns were built in 178 BC to replace the old ionian columns. Three of these brinth columns remain also today. The Gallery floor was made in such a way to enable the patients' barefoot walking, lying and resting on the floor. It is assumed that the wooden roof was covered with tiles, made of earth or marble.

A Roman theatre with a capacity of 3500 spectators was built at the southwest corner of the north Partikos. The theatre which was constructed by dressing the stones is semi-circular. To protect the theatre from leaking, a canal was dug by drilling the stones at the base. This canal that supports the theatre from inside has two exits on both sides. By this the humidity is avoided by providing air circulation.

There are two doors that connect the theatre to the northern gallery. At the top of the theatre, there is a gallery, surrounding the theatre which has ionian columns. In the middle there is a diazoma. There is an honor box in the first section, right accross the stage. People having high status used to sit there. The orchestra is ornamented by colorful marsles and is in a semi-circular shape.

The Western Wall with Columns
Columns of Corinth (down)

Asklepion Theater (up) and its Side Entrances (down)

The stage is 1 meter high and is marble covered. Once there was a three-floored building with statues between the niches at the theatre. But today, only some fundamentals and some architectural pieces remain.

The west Partikos, extending from the theatre to the Catrina is 95 meters long. This marble gallery, that resembles the northern one has ion headed columns on three stairs as well. The floor and the walls are covered with colorful marbles. There is a stoa, 93 m. long made of andesit stone, in Doric style.

This place was built on the west side outside the Asklepion, Sacred Area in Hellenistic Age. The ruins belonging to that period are found here. It is also assumed that the Sacred Gymnasion where Aristeides used to lie down and rest, existed here. In the southern gallery, there is a room near the stages going up the gallery. Why this room is constructed, can not be explained. At the end of the southern gallery, there is a toilet and a meeting room. The toilet which is below the gallery level, has two rooms. The larger room is for men and the smaller is used by woman. The roof of the larger room is fitted on four korinth columns.

Some space is left in the middle to let air and light in. The large room is for 40 people and the smaller can be used by 17. Due to the sloping ground, the seating places and other parts are made of marble. As there is no resistive earth and rock layers, basement was built by drilling deep foundations. An ionic gallery is built on this layer... At this large area three small temples and Asklepion are found. These structures were surrounded by galleries during the Roman Empire period.

Resting rooms and gardens in front are restored many times in history. In Roman period, they remained at their previous places.

Asclepieion Western Stoa (up)
Latrine (down)

There is a sacred fountainhead and a pool in the large area beside these structures. The sacred fountain-head somewhere towards the west of the area's north corridor is followed by pipes to the water cistern. This pool is in the middle of the large area. The wall which is built beside the stairs leading to the square shaped pool aids to rise the water level and keep outside clean. It is also probable, that this pool was covered by a roof. There is another pool in between the western corridor and rocks. Aristeidos used to have his mud-baths here.

In Roman Period, another marble coated pool was built in the large area. There were four stairs descending to the pool which had 3.40 to 22.5 ms. measures. The patients used to sit on the stairs under the sun, after having their baths in the pool. Drinking water used to came from outside through lead pipes. This pool appears to be an outdoor pool with only a marble railing around. There is a sacred well at the bottom of the marble pool. The water for this pool was taken from this well. Water used to boil in different levels inside the well. As the water reached the necessary level, remaining water ran directly to the pool.

The overflowing water runs down a canal of 9 meters length beneath Kriptoportikos. In the middle of the big courtyard, beside the sacred fountainhead there is a vaulted underground road (Kriptportikus) of 80 meters length which can be reached by 16 stairs down. This basement narrows from the north to the south; over the basement there are 12 windows with certain distances, which lets air and light in. When it was necessary, these windows were covered by stone covers. The base of the basement is covered with well-adorned large stones. There is a water canal running through in the middle, beneath this instalment. This canal which was constructed with caving rocks has a connection with the others that collects the water at the Main Area, and then it gives the water to the second canal running down. The sound of the slowly running water was used to soothe mentally disturbed people. The patients were able to come down to the lower part without facing any disturbance of traught.

People can get into this building through Kriptportikus as well as by the stairs coming down from the Main Area. This two floored (circular) round building is supported by many water canal systems and is made of vault-covered monumental passage and pools. The base of the structure is set on the dressed rocks at the north-east side and the other parts are supported.

A terrace for sunbathing was added in the south. The water canals beneath the building were used to bring drinking water and to let the rain water, which comes to the stream in the south from the upper floor.

The building was covered with marble sheets. There was a staircase at the south, leading to the upper floor, which was completely ruined. There are six big apsis at this flat. The room was made of wood and tiles.

This round (circular) shaped building was built after on other round (circular) shaped temple which was made in the name of Asklepios. By the stairs at the south side of the round (circular) building, it is passed to a peristyled structure. This peristyle house was built in Roman Period (Age). At the courtyard of the building is a pool covered with marble sheets. Asklepios stands at the west of the peristyle building and at the south of Propy. This round shaped temple was built as the Panthean model that was made by Emperor Hadrianus in Rome, but half as big.

Panthean was built 20 years later, it was made by the consul C.Rufmus and donated

Peristyle House

in 142 B.C. The building has an entrance with columns and stairs, and through this it is entered to the temple.

Inside the building, seven wall niches, semicircled and cornered, are lined up.

There is cult statue of Asklepios, the god of health, at the niche accross the entrance. The roof has a diameter of 20.85 meters. Inner side of the roof is covered with colourful mosaics; there is a space in the middle. The base of this building still remains.

The asklelpieion, which was protected against air currents, with its healing waters, its corridors for walking, theatre, library, treatment places and temples, was the most important health center of its time. In Asklepieion there were very famous doctors such as Calos, Antipas, Galenos, Nikomadez, Flavius and Heteider.

The Emperor Caracalla, the orator Aristeides were some of the people who gained their health back in Asklepieion.

Cure House (up)
Down Round Building (down)

AMPHITHEATRE

The most remarkable structures of the Roman Empire Period are Stadion, Lower City Theatre and Amphitheatre on the hill between the Acropolis and Asklepieion.

Although the drilling excavation and researches are made partly in the area where these structures stand, a detailed excavation has not been made yet. The Amphitheatre represents an example of a rare structure in Anatolia. The base, the vaulted passages and columns of this structure of which the excavation has not been made, still remains.

Remainders of the Amphitheater

Remainders of the Amphitheater

TUMULI

There are a lot of Tumuli (Hill Graves) on the Kaikes plain. A few of them are within the modern Pergamon structures. Looking over the Acropolis towards the south, the hill graves scattered around the plain can be seen. The largest ones are the tumuli of Maltepe, Yığmatepe and Tavşantepe. Among them, only the tumulus of Maltepe was opened and robbed in the earlier periods. In 1900, the grave room was entered from the door in the western part and the plan of the room was made. 45 meter corridor beyond the vaulted door intersects with a second corridor which has a length of 17 meters. There are 3 grave rooms, opening out to the second corridor. No definite information could be acquired about Yığmatepe and Tavşantepe tumuli because they were not dug out. Between 1905 and 1909 drilling processes were carried out in the name of German Archaeological Institute with the chairmanship of Prof. Dörpfield. But they were not concluded because of frequent erosions.

THE BERGAMA MUSEUM

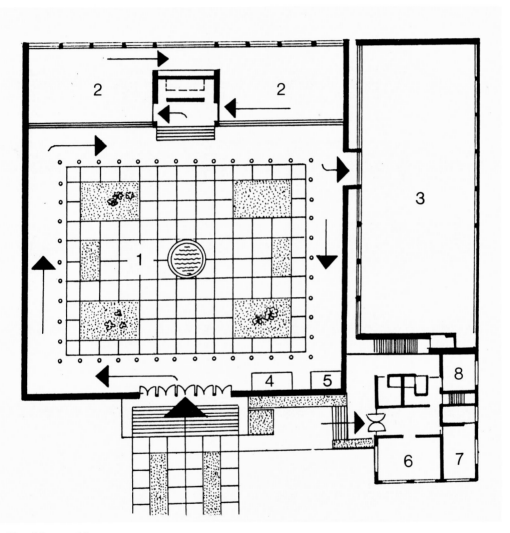

The Plan of Bergama Museum:

1- Interior Yard.
2- Archeology Hall
3- Ethnology Hall
4- Stand
5-Café
6-Manager
7-Museum officer
8-Etude Room

The excavations in Bergama Acropolis were started in 1878, under the supervision of Carl Humann. During the second part of these excavations lead between 1900-1913, under the supervision of Wilhelm Dörpfeld, an archaeological depot museum was established in the place where the German excavation house is located today. This depot museum is one of the two archaeological depot museums established in Turkey at the beginning of the 20th century.

Later on, in 1924, with Osman Bayatlı's contributions, the first museum was founded in Bergama, in Public Education Central Building.

The excavations which were halted during World War I, were started again in 1927, under Theodor Wiegond's supervision. Since the excavations in Acropolis and in Asklepion were started in the same period, the necessity of a new museum emerged. General Fevzi Çakmak who visited Bergama in 1932, dealt with this subject and ordered the establishment of a new museum. For the place of the building, which was planned to be constructed with Turkish-German cooperation, an old cemetery was found suitable. The building was planned by Bruno Meyer and Harold Hanson. The project was finished in 1932. According to the project, the museum building would be constructed in such a way that it would be surrounded by galleries. It would be consisted of a rectangular courtyard and of an exhibition hall. The galeries of the courtyard were thought to serve as an open-air museum. The place between the street and the museum was planned to be a front garden with stairs over the three terraces. On both sides of the building, enough space would be left for possible additions.

In 1933, the basic x construction was started by the Governor of İzmir, Kazım Dirik. When Kemal Atatürk visited Bergama on 13.4.1934, the construction was still going on. The museum building which was finished on 30 October 1936 was opened to public by Fazlı Güleç, Governor of Izmir. On 23.2.1937, prime minister İsmet İnönü made an official visit to the museum.

A photograph showing İsmet İnönü with Osman Bayatlı in front of the museum and his thanking words in the museum book can be seen also today.

Osman Bayatlı who founded the first Ethnographic Museum of Turkey in Bergama and who made great contributions to the establishment of the archaeological museum, died on April 15, 1958. Until his death, he collected materials for both etnographic and archaeological museums and worked for their exhibitions in the best possible way.

In 1979, a hall was added to the building for the exhibition of etnographic materials, collected by Osman Bayatlı. The etnographic museum which was a part of the Public Education Building until that day, was moved to the hall in the archaeological museum. The museum was then enlarged with the addition of depots, library, working and office rooms to it.

Most of the archaeological materials that are now exhibited in the museum, were brought about by German archaeologists during the excavations made in Acropolis, Asklepieion, Serapeion (Red courtyard) "Musalla cemeteries in Bergama. Some of them are the pieces that were brought about by Turkish archaeologists during the excavations in ancient Gryneion (New Şakran), Ketios (Kestel) (it was behind the Bergama Acropolis) and in ancient Pitane (Çandarlı). Other findings from Pergamon are also exhibited in the museum.

The pieces exhibited in the museum are placed in order, according to their historical dates and particularities. At the entrance of the museum, in the lower terrace of the outer garden, tombs, ostotekhes and phalluses are placed on the right side. These pieces most of which were found in the cemetery on the sides of Acropolis, belong to the Hellenistic and Roman ages. To the left of the lower terrace, there are pillar heads, pillar body parts and pillar tombs. These pieces belong to the Roman period.

In the second terrace of the outer garden, architectural pieces, grave inscriptions, ostotekhes, big cubes, pillar heads and parts and sculptural works are exhibited. On the

Asklepion Western Stoa (up)
Latrine (down)

left side of the second terrace, there is a place containing Islamic grave stones and tombs. They were brought from the Musalla cemetery.

At the entrance of the interior garden of the museum, on the left hand side, the thin fresque on the wall was brought about during the excavations in Acropolis. It belongs to the 2nd century B.C.

At the entrance of the interior garden of the museum, on the left hand side, the thin fresque on the wall was brought about during the excavations in Acropolis. It belongs to the 2nd century B.C.

The tomb at the entrance to the interior garden of the museum is a child's grave. It was excavated during Ketios (Kestel) excavations. In the entrance, in the gallery on the left side of the interior garden, there are architectural pieces dating back to Hellenistic, Roman and Byzantine ages. Most of these pieces were brought from Athena Sacred Area, Zeus' altar, Dionysos Temple and Asklepieion. These places were all in Acropolis. Apart from them, the pillar heads found in Acropolis and Asklepieion are also exhibited in that gallery. Also in the left gallery, there is a copy of the Zeus' altar the original parts of which are being exhibited in East Berlin today. The original statue belongs to the first half of 2nd century B.C. (180-160 B.C.) The sculptural works in the altar are the most beautiful samples of the Bergama sculptural school. The pathetic expression on the face of the statues, the baro-ue style and realism in their clothes, hair, beard and muscles are the most important properties of **Pergamon** sculpture.

Before entering the archaeology exhibition hall, to the left of the gallery, there are statues and grave steles of the Hellenistic age. They mostly reflect the properties of Bergama sculpture. The statues on the right side of the entrance belong to the Roman age and they possess the same properties. In the gallery at the right side of the museum garden, there are laws and several inscriptions about the Pergamon kingdom, which show the social and economical life of Pergamon at Roman times.

A Freize of Demeter Temple (up)
Tomb Steles (down)
An Architectural Part (bottom)

The Helios Stele-2 nd Century A.D. (up)

The Marble Altar (down)

The "Alınlık", "Akroter" figures of Asklepieion Propylon are known as the most famous works in Bergama museum, but it is thought that they previously served as the "Akreter" of Dionysos temple in Acropolis, then were brought to Asklepieion from there. They belong to the Roman age. Besides these works, pillar heads and torsos of Byzantian age are also exhibited in the garden.

At the entrance of the Archaeological Exhibition Hall, there is a cross statue which was found in ancient Pitane (Çandarlı) city. This restored work is of 6th century B.C. In the exhibition hall, at the left side of the entrance, there are ceramic and terracotta works.

The oldest ceramics, exhibited in the museum are of ancient Bronze age (2450-2150 B.C.) They are exhibited in two windows. In one of the windows there are Pitane ceramics, where as in the other window there are ceramics of Hellenistic, Roman and Byzantian ages that were mostly made in Bergama ateliers. These ateliers were found during the excavations made in Ketios (Kestel). The ceramics of Archaic age that were excavated in Gryneion (New Şakran) and the Myrine terracotas (2nd-1st centuries B.C.) are exhibited the two windows standing next to each other. Bronze works (of Roman age), the statues of Goddess Kybele, glass and bone neclaces, bracelets and medical equipments are exhibited in the windows of the left ehibition hall. Another important work exhibited in this hall is the golden chariot relief of Hellenistic age. The ceramics of Byzantine age can be seen in the window on the right side of the hall entrance.

In showcases, at the entrance to the right side of the exhibition hall, oil lamps dating back to the Roman age, bronze motives symbolizing the gods of health, Asklepios and Asklepieion, metal works, coins belonging to the period between Archaic age and Roman age, and the ceramics found in Kestel excavations are being exhibited. Although the portait of the philosopher Socrates (of Roman age) and the statue of Apollon Kitharoidos reflect the effect of the 6th century B.C. art technique, they belong to the Antonins period because of the decorations and the upper face formations

Nike Top Acroter-Roman Period (up)
Cyros Statue-6th C. A.C. (down)

Ceramic Cups - Hellenistic Period

on them. Together with the portrait of the historian Xenophon (of Roman age), these three can be regarded as the most important marble works of that period.

In the exhibition hall, to the right of the entrance, there are more marble works. The most important piece, there, is the statue of Emperor Hadrianus. This statue was found in the library during the Asklepieion excavations. In the statue, which has a colossal form, Emperor Hadrianus was carved naked. The pathetic expression on his face is a characteristic of Bergama Sculpture School that also continued in Roman age. The statue dated back to 2nd century A.D.

In the right exhibition hall, there are the marble portraits of Emperor Vespasianus (I.C. A.D.), Emperor Hadrianus (II. C. A.D.), Emperor Caracalla (III. C. A.D.) and of Euripides (of Roman age)

The portrait of Diodoros Pasparos which was found in the marble hall near the Odeion during the Acropolis excavations is also exhibited here. He was known to be a powerful man in Bergama who lived in the years 70's B.C. He was so powerful that the was respected like a God. The reliefs about him are found near the big mosaic ornamentation on the ground. The subjects worked on them are: a fight cock, a helmet, a star which aids to the success of Dioskurs, a sword and an armour.

In the mosaic ornamentations on the floor, there is a Medusa head which is surrounded by geometric decorations. This mosaic which was given as a present by Fehmi Kural, a Bergama lawyer, during the construction of the museum, was dated 3rd century B.C.

In the showcases of the right of the exhibition hall, there are earthenware statues, glass works and little marble works. Among these little marble works, an Eros head which dates back to 1st centruy A.D. is being exhibited. The characteristics of Bergama Sculpture School are seen in Eros which was designed as a child. Under the exhibition window, there is a relief showing two people and two chariots.

Terra Cotta Oil Lamp - Roman Period   The Golden Ear Relief - Hellenistic Period

Some Archeological Expressions:

ABSID: Buckled salient located behind naves in the churches or basilicas.
AKROTER: Base located on top or sides of a front plate, carrying a sculpture and ornament piece.
ALKOV: A room assigned for worship alone.
ANTA: Short salient wall built on building sides, and especially in the temples.
AUDITORIUM: Place of meeting at public shows, in the ancient Greek and Roman buildings.
DIAZOMA: Horizontal passage along the seat rows in the Theatre Cavea.
EKSEDRA: Salient place or Alkov, type half circle where elevated seats are located.
EPISTYL: Name of the head-base blocks situated on the columns.
FRIEZE: Lateral section between the corniches and the head-base on the eaves.
HYPOKAUST: Underbase heating system.
CAVEA: Theater auditorium.
NAOS: Main room (Cell) where God sculptures are preserved in Greek temples.
NECCORUS: Temple assigned to the Emperor for worship and the city where this temple is located.
NYMPHAEUM: Structure ornamented with sculptures, vases and fountains, devoted to Nymphes are known as water, forest and mountain fairies in ancient Greek literature.
ODEION: Small structure like a theatre, employed for recitals and dramas.
PALASTRA: Open courtyard employed for athletics.
PERYDOLOS: Surrounding wall around the temple walls.
PODIUM: Smooth, sound base situated under structures or structure elements.
PORTIC: Open corridor covered by a roof and ending with columns.
PRONAOS: Front room in the temples, facing west in general.
PROPYLON: Monumental structure located on front of palaces, temples or cities in the ancient Greek civilizations.
SELLA: Main room where the worship sculpture is located in the temples.
SKENE: Scene of the ancient Greek theatres.
STYLOBAT: Stone basis situated under a column row.
STOA: Column row covered with a roof.
TETRASTOON: A rectangular area surrounded by four stoas or column rows.

Nike-Hellenistic Period

A Sitting woman Statue - Hellenistic Period

A woman statue-1 st. century A.D.

The terra cotta statuette of a boy - 2 nd. century A.D.

102

The Tyche Statue - 1st. C. A.D. (right)

Statue of a Man
Centaurus - Hellenistic Period

The Statue of a Woman
The Statue of a Woman - Hellenistic Period

Hermes Carrying Child Dionysos - 1st C. A.D. (right)

Statue of a sitting woman.

Apollon Statue - Roman Period

Dyonysos and The Smiling Kid - Roman Period

Kybele Statuette - Roman Period

The Statue of Emperor Hadrianus 2 nd C. A.D.

Portrait of Emperor Hadrianus - 2 nd Century A.D.

Emperor Vespasianus- 1 st Century A.D.

The Bust of a Man - 3 rd Century A.D.

Socrates Head - Roman Period

Athena Head - Hellenistic Period (right)

Head of a Woman - Roman Period
The Bust of Europides - Roman Period

Head of a Woman
The Smiling Child (Eros) - 2 nd century A.D.

ETHNOGRAPHY HALL

It is possible to see the most beautiful examples of Turkish-Islamic Art in Ethnography Hall where Bergama carpets, kilims, linen or cotton weavings and also handscrafts belong to the other region of Anatolia have been exhibited.

Before we tell you the ethnographic works exhibited in the Ethnography Hall, we'd like to tell shortly the weaving in Bergama region.

There weren't any houses without having loom in Bergama and its villages by the end of the nineteenth century. There were carpet looms and cotton cloth in almost every houses. Clipped wool was carded, spinned, and carpet and kilim were weaved. In the houses, cotton was made "mahlıç", spinned in spinning looms, and white, motley cloths were weaved.

Today, in Bergama, cloth weaving has disappeared completely but, still, weaving has been making in the downtown and some villages for Tourism purposes.

There are Bergama carpets and kilims at the left side of the enter of Ethnograpy Hall. Yurtdağ, Yağcıbedir and Kozak carpets, kilims and weavings, belong to XVIII. and XIX. centuries, have same features. The main colours of these carpets and kilims, belong to Bergama, red, dark blue and white. Additional colours are green, orange, yellow and claret red. The geometric shapes in these carpets and kilims are old feature.

The base colour of "Bergama Prayer Rug" is violet-pink, ledge colour is dark and geometric shapes, which are violet-pink, silver, cover on them. The colours of middle part of the rug are light blue and green. Same colour has been used for every motives.

There are two medals each in the bottom and upper sides of middle part and also there are two medals each in the bottom and upper sides of the rug. There are star, horizontal, triangle, baklava and flowers motives on the base.

Yunddağ is the south of Bergama. It is the weaving center with its famous "Tabaklı" carpets. The base of the carpet is divided into eight squares. The other kind of carpet is a rug known as "İbrikli" The motives of an old İbrikli carpet include that a mihrab in the center, a flower vase in the mihrab, an almond in the "Seymen", a star with eight corners, a holly mirror in the middle, a case under the mihrab and four oranges which are cut in it and "Göynek" Embroidery under the case. (This embroidery has been in "Yörük Göyneks" too.

Kozak is the north of Bergama. Since Kozak carpets have wide ledges, they have some similarities between Dakıcı carpets and them. There is a part in which verses from Koran have been in "Kozak Prayer Rugs."

Kilims which are weaved in Kozak are called according to motives on them such as Sandık (case), Havuzbaşı (pool corner), Tarak (comb), Çayırçiçeği (timothy grass), Payam, Gümüşçengel, Keçitüğmez, Benli (spotted), Savran, Armutçiçeği (pear flower), Ördekzülfü, Bölükyürek (Broken heart). Sacks are called such as Kestane Yaprağı (Chestnut leaf), Elekyüzü, Farda, Koziçi, Deveboynu (neck of camel), Kapıkolu (door handle), Taka (a small boat), Tırnak (nail), Balık (fish), Göz (Eye) and Çınaryaprağı (plane tree leaf). Saddlebags are called such as Sulu (watered), Elekyüzü, Al (red), Tarak (comb) and Uykulama (sleeping).

Yağcıbedir is the east of Bergama. Kocaoba village is the weaving center of this region. There are prayer rugs which are named as "Obanamazlası", "Karagöznamazla", "Yapraklı (sarı) namazla" (Leafed (yellow)). This carpet has 4x5 nodes in one centimeter square. In addition, types of "Fincanlı", "Koçelmalı", "Minareli" have

Carpet Weaving Bench

been weaven in this areas. "The Amulet motif" is seen as a characteristic motif in Bergama carpets. The type of the node is "Gördes". Aniline dye has mostly been used in Kozak and Yunddağ weavings whereas vegetable dye has been used in Yağcıbedir weavings. So, Yağcıbedir weavings are more valuable because their colours never fade. Yunddağ and Kozak carpets, which have been exhibited in the museum have same features too. Vegetable dyes have been known by the people but not used today. The raw materials of them are oak bark for brown and black colour; valonia oak for black; Pomegranete bark for brown and black; hazelnut bark for brown; madder for wine colour; pot dye for dark blue; grape leaf for bright green.

Tools related to weaving such as cloth-weaving loom, spinning loom are in the enter of Hall. Shepherd goods and clothes and various madders have been exhibited in glass cases at the left side of the enter. Kilims, carpets, weaven saddlebags, sacks have been displayed on the panels in this section. Carpet and kilim looms are simple. These looms consist of two side woods, two lower-upper round woods, two warping blocks, two lower-upper bend poles. Kirkit, scissors, blade, two strechers, wool warping and filling are useful for weaving. A cotton cloth loom consists of two side woods on four legs, two front-back ulama woods, two warping reed on two legs. It is used for weaving the threads such as filling, masır, çımbar.

Wool clothweaving warping ano filling are called as "Kırpıt". They have been boiled by beating. They are good garments for winter. Orient Corner, which is in Ethnography Hall, has been decorated as an old Turkish house where copper kitchen utensiles, clothweavings, saltshaker,

A view from Etnography Hall.

Orient Corner (bottom)

napkins, wooden and boxwood spoons have been exhibited. In this corner, also, Turkish musical instruments such as divan saz, cura, zilli maşa, darbuka (a kind of small drum), def (a tambourine with cymbals) and kaval (shepherd's pipe).

There are samples on the panels from various regions of Anatolia, except Bergama kilims and carpets, including Kayseri, Çanakkale, Nevşehir, Tokat, Sivas, Kars Kırşehir, Gördes kilims and carpets which are the most beautiful works of the Hall.

Throughout the history, while Turks gave great importance on woman garment and also they have large materials in this subject. Garments in glass cases are the most beautiful samples of them. This is very important because they show Anatolian women's artistic ability and fastidiousness.

We can find sometimes culture units of Anatolia or sometimes regional features in these garments. An integrity is seen between the Harbalı and Üçetek garment embroidered with square technique on velvet and bride garment, inner garments and jewellery on neck.

At another glass case, Türkmen, Çepni and Alevi bride garments are exhibited with their specific style, colours, embroiders, weaving and cap on the head, waist and even stocking.

Hand crafts and "Oya" embroidery which have a specific role in Turkish arts are so important in Bergama just like as other Anatolian cities. "Oya" art is fully specific to Turkish arts. This is proven by the fact that "Oya" word has no equivalent in other languages. "Oya" embroidery displayed in the glass cases and boards in the etnography hall is interesting in terms of representing the regional features of Turkish hand crafts prepared by Turkish young girls.

Besides the foregoing products, there are traces of harness, jewellery, vapor cups, writing assemblies, coloured glass lamps, coffee mills, timber make-up bags, "Efe" garments and weapons in the glass cases. The displayed weapons belong the soldiers of "National Struggle" of Turkish people.

Bergama carpet prayer rug, woolen, 19 th Century (right)

Prayer rug, Bergama - Yağcıbedir

Prayer rug, Bergama - Yağcıbedir

Silk embroidery (oya) with grape bunch patterns

Silk embroidery (oya) with Bird patterns

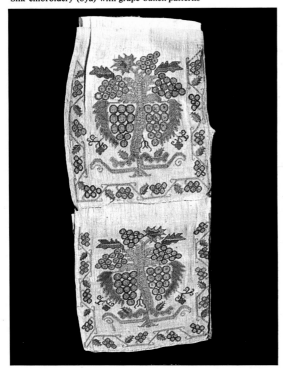

Woolen bags
Silver belts

A bride headdress
A regional embroidered skirt.

Oil lamp

Darbuka (a kind of hand drum)

Wooden make-up box, 18 th century

Zurna (oboe like music instrument)

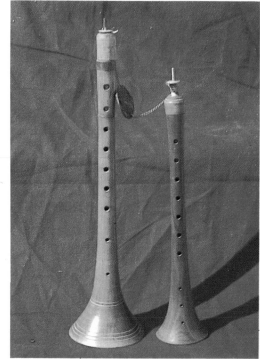

BIBLIOGRAPHY

- İlhan AKŞİT, Batı Anadolu Uygarlığı-İSTANBUL 1980
- Oktay AKŞİT, Roma İmparatorluk Tarihi (M.Ö. 27-M.S. 192) İSTANBUL 1976
- Oktay AKŞİT, Roma İmparatorluk Tarihi, (M.S. 193-393) İSTANBUL 1970
- Ekrem AKURGAL, Ancient Civilizations and Ruins of Turkey 5. Baskı-İSTANBUL 1984
- Necip ALTINIŞIK, Bergama'da Eski Türk Yapıları İZMİR 1982
- Remzi Oğuz ARIK, L'histoire et L'organisation des Musees Turcs İSTANBUL
- Sabahat ATLAN, Roma Tarihinin Ana Hatları İSTANBUL 1970
- Osman BAYATLI, Bergama Tarihinde İlk Çağ İSTANBUL 1949
- Osman BAYATLI, Bergama'da Krallık Devri İSTANBUL 1950
- Osman BAYATLI, Bergama'da Sanat Eserleri ve Abideleri İSTANBUL 1951
- Osman BAYATLI, Bergama'da Asklepion İZMİR 1947
- Osman BAYATLI, Küplü Hamam İSTANBUL 1942
- Osman BAYATLI, Bergama Tarihinde Türk-İslam Eserleri İSTANBUL 1956
- Osman BAYATLI, Bergama'da Karaosman Oğullarından Mehmet Ağa Vakfı İZMİR
- Gottfried GRUBEN, Die Tempel der Griechen MÜNCHEN-HİRMER 1980
- Şadan GÖKOVALI, Bergama-İZMİR
- Doğan HASOL, Ansiklopedik Mimarlık Sözlüğü Haziran 1975
- Herodotos, Herodot Tarihi (Türkçesi Müntekim ÖKMEN) İSTANBUL 1973
- Homeros, İliada (Çeviren: Ahmet Cevat EMRE) İSTANBUL IV. Baskı 1971
- Homeros, Odysseia (Çeviren Ahmet Cevat EMRE) İSTANBUL 1971
- İslam Ansiklopedisi, 6. Cilt M.E.B. İSTANBUL 1967
- Naci KEKEÇ Bergama'da Osmanlı Dönemi Dini Mimarisi (Yayınlanmamış Öğrenim Tezi) ERZURUM 1986
- Tevhit KEKEÇ, ''Bergama'nın Eski Su Yolları'' Arkeoloji ve Sanat Dergisi Sayı 22/23
- Doğan KUBAN, Mimarlık Kavramları İSTANBUL 1980
- Arif Müfit MANSEL, Ege ve Yunan Tarihi ANKARA 1971
- Klaus NOHLEN und Wolfgang RADT''KAPIKAYA'' Altertümer von Pergamon XII BERLİN 1978
- Mehmet ÖZSAİT, Hellenistik ve Roma Devrinde Pisidya Tarihi İSTANBUL 1987
- İsmet PARMAKSIZOĞLU, İbn BATUTA Seyahatnamesinden Seçmeler İSTANBUL 1971
- Adnan PEKMAN, Strabon-Coğrafya Anadolu (Kitap. XII. XIII. XIV) Arkeoloji ve Sanat Yayınları İSTANBUL 1987
- Wolfgang RADT, Bergama Arkeolojik Rehber İSTANBUL 1984
- Wolfgang RADT, ''Pergamon Grabungeskampagne im Herbst 1972-Vorbericht'' Türk Arkeoloji Dergisi Sayı: XXI/2 ANKARA 1974
- Wolfgang RADT, ''Bergama Müzesinin Yapılışı. Atatürk Devrinde Türk-Alman İşbirliğine Bir Örnek'' T.T.K. ANKARA 1986
- Cemil TOKSÖZ, Ancient Cities of Western Anatolia İSTANBUL 1979
- Cemil TOKSÖZ, A.travel Quide to the Historic Treasures of Turkey İSTANBUL 1977
- Türk Ansiklopedisi, Cilt: 6 (M.E.B.) İSTANBUL 1968
- Sebahattin TÜRKOĞLU - Erol ATALAY, Efes (II. Baskı) İZMİR 1978
- Adem VAROL, Bergama'da Osmanlı Dönemi profan Mimarisi (Yayınlanmamış-Öğrenci Tezi) ERZURUM 1985
- Muhsin YENİM, Pergame-A travels les ages İZMİR 1972
- R.E.WYCHERLEY, Antik Çağda Kentler Nasıl Kuruldu. (Çeviri, Nur NİRVEN-Nezih BAŞGELEN) İSTANBUL 1986

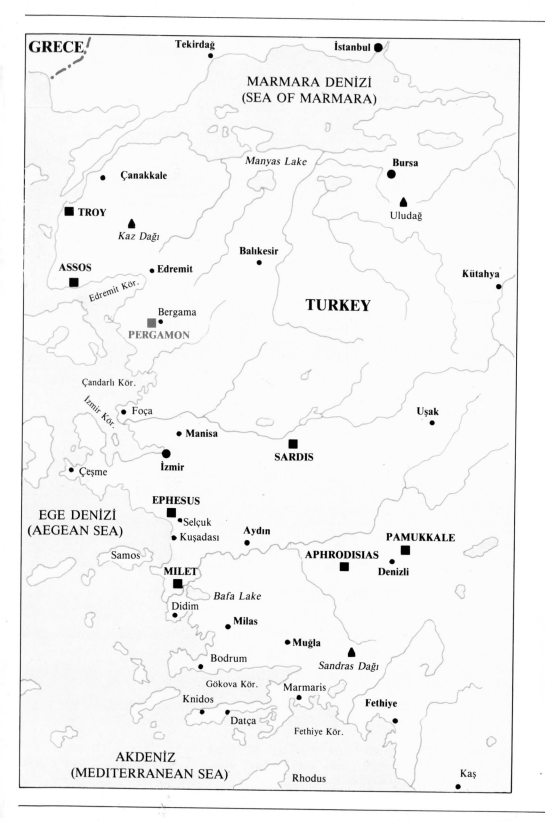